MOTHER TRAUMA

Running from, Fighting with, and
Refusing to Repeat the Deepest Betrayal

Mother Trauma

Emily Lewis Bowers

LIONCREST
PUBLISHING

MOTHER TRAUMA

Running From, Fighting with, and Refusing to Repeat the Deepest Betrayal

FIRST EDITION

ISBN   978-1-5445-2846-5   *Hardcover*
      978-1-5445-2845-8   *Paperback*
      978-1-5445-2844-1   *Ebook*
      978-1-5445-2847-2   *Audiobook*

This book is dedicated to my children:
Zechariah, Harper, and Otto.

Love, Mom

Contents

Introduction

JANUARY 2021, TWO DAYS BEFORE MY THIRTY-FOURTH birthday. I log in to Facebook, and a memory from ten years ago pops up. It's a picture of Jill and me. The caption reads "Me and Mom." That's all. I smile, remembering the day the photo was taken. So many happy memories of my mom, and many more to come. Over the years, Jill has become not only my mother but also a surrogate grandmother to my three young children. No, not a surrogate. She is their real grandma—a woman who showers them with love and attention, just like any real grand-mother would do. Jill makes my children feel loved. Just like she has done for me.

I smile again, this time at the thought of having someone in my children's lives who loves them like I do, like my husband, their father Brent, does. Children need a lot of love. People need love. I repost the memory on Facebook. It's one of my favorites.

* * *

It's been a busy morning, but now I can relax. The kids are fed, and they're down in the basement playroom. They have a tent and sleeping bags to play in, along with blocks and all sorts of toys. I can hear little Otto's favorite toy, the musical one that plays songs about animals. I can hear Zech's and Harper's voices too. The kids have a good time together, so I'll leave them alone and enjoy the peace for a while. The kitchen's clean, the dishes are done. Brent's left for work. I check out Facebook and see that my reposted memory has lots of likes and emojis and a few comments from friends. Social media can be good some days. Some days.

Among the sweet words is another comment. It's from Sadie, who's related to me through my biological mother, Jennie. I barely know Sadie, but due to the nature of social media, I've accepted her online friendship at some point. She's an aunt or a second cousin or something. I'm not even sure. All I know is her comment does not belong on my memory.

Oh Emily, it reads, *That's not your mom.*

That comment, those words. *Why? Why would anyone feel the need to write something like that on my memory? Why would Sadie think that was okay?* I'm feeling a lot of things right now. I want to defend Jill, my mom. I also want to tell Sadie to butt out of my business. A moment ago I was happy, and now I'm angry, and it's not fair that someone's rudeness can ruin my day. I have to let it go for now. I'll put it aside and respond when I've had time to think.

A couple of hours later, I type my response. It's polite but firm. I don't engage in arguments online. I also don't let people push me around. I gently remind Sadie that Jill's been there for me since I was an adolescent. She helped raise me, loved me, showed me what it was like to be in a healthy mother-daughter relationship. Yes, I know she didn't actually give birth to me.

She's not my biological mom. I'm keenly aware of that fact. But in every other way, she has been a mother to me—shown me true, unconditional, motherly love. To me, that's had a greater impact on my life—a more *positive* impact—than all the negative memories I have of my biological mom, Jennie. I didn't have a choice when I was a child, but as an adult, I choose love over trauma. Over cruelty. Over shame. I choose Jill as my mom, and no words on social media or anywhere else can change that. I don't write all of that in my Facebook comment. I keep it short—make my point and move on with the day.

* * *

It's the next day, the day before my birthday. I have a private message on Facebook. It's from Sadie, and it's long. She's calling me out, telling me I was wrong to post that photo saying Jill is my mom. Sadie claims that Jennie was around for me when I was little and that she clearly remembers her raising me and being a good mom. *Really? I saw this woman, Sadie, twice when I was growing up. What does she know about my life? About Jennie?*

Then she says that she's heard all the stories about me, that Jennie's filled her in on what really happened. She doesn't come out and say it, but she's insinuating that she knows my story better than I do. It goes on, and here's the part that really makes my blood boil.

Sadie says that it's my job to rebuild a relationship with my "real" mother, Jennie. That my brothers and I should take it upon ourselves to reconnect with her. That we should take responsibility for the past and make amends. She's blaming me for what happened. Blaming my brothers too. And blaming us for not fixing our broken family.

Under the anger, I sort of get it. She's a relative of Jennie's, and they no doubt had a very different relationship than I had with my biological mother. She loves this woman and is defending her. I write back, telling her that I appreciate her standing up for Jennie, but no, it's not my job to fix the relationship. Jennie was the adult. She created the chaos and caused the damage. It's not up to me to make amends. I'm an adult now, with my own children to take care of—to be a real mother to.

Thank you for the message, I write, and *have a nice day.*

I have to let this go. I don't want it to spoil my day. And I can let go of it—most of it. But one thing just won't go away. The idea that someone thinks they know my story better than I do. That someone has this distorted picture of what I went through, the life I lived.

I'm in the shower, washing my hair, and I can't get this thought out of my head: *I have to tell my story.*

So began my journey to write this book. I started talking to people about my story and discovered I wasn't the only woman with "mommy issues." Other women, even among my friends, were also dealing with the deep betrayal of a mother who couldn't—or simply refused to—love her children. A mother who didn't comfort them, nurture them, or provide a safe and stable homelife. A mother who caused pain, anxiety, uncertainty, and fear. A mother who was the antithesis of what a young girl needs.

My desire to tell my story wasn't about spite, anger, or being right. After years of dealing with my mommy issues the wrong way, I've learned to break the cycle. I've become the mom I wish I had so my own children won't suffer the pain that I endured. But I want other women to know that they're not the only ones who've been through this, and there is another way to live. That they can get healthy, have good relationships with other women, with men, with their families. That the mother you were born with doesn't have to be the mother you love.

* * *

Hi. I'm Emily. I live in a small town in Florida, and for the past six years, I've been a stay-at-home mom, which is the best job in the world.

I have three sweet children, an amazing husband, two wonderful brothers, and a father I adore. I have friends—women who care about me, listen to me, and trust me with their secrets. I trust them too. Then there's Jill, a woman I've unofficially, but with all of my heart and soul, adopted as my mom.

There are good people in my life, and I'm grateful for every one of them.

I also have a biological mother named Jennie.

It's hard to write this, even now, after all the talk therapy and the healing. The forgiveness. People aren't supposed to say bad things about their mothers. Moms have the hardest jobs. They not only bring new life into the home—they hold the family together. Mothers are sources of light and hugs, kisses and love. A lot of love. We put moms on a pedestal because that's where they belong. But not all moms. Because some moms are not all these things. Some moms come from families where trauma is passed down from one generation to the next. Households where yelling and shaming and harsh words and cruelty are the norm.

So how do we deal with those moms? How do we broach the subject without feeling judged? Or being seen as ungrateful? Without feeling shame—for where we came from and how we're handling it? It's not easy, but in this book, I'm going to try. Because I was raised in a home with a mother who wasn't any of those things a mom is supposed to be. My mother was verbally and emotionally abusive, and it affected me. I had no idea how much until I was an adult. And I had to work very hard to heal myself, to learn to trust, to love. To be a good mother to my own children. And even though it may be taboo to talk about mothers with anything but glowing praise, I'm going to tell the truth—my truth about my mother.

I changed some people's names in the book to protect their privacy. This isn't a work of vindictiveness. It's not meant to hurt other people. I wrote this book for myself because I know my story—I lived it. And I want to set the record straight. I wrote it for my husband so he'll understand me a little better, and for my children, so when they're old enough, they'll understand me better too. I wrote it for any woman who's dealing with mother trauma. And for young girls who are living it right now.

I'm not a therapist, or a counselor, or a psychologist. I'm a woman who's been through some things. You might see yourself in my story. You might see a friend in my story, or a relative. If you were raised in a home of mother trauma, I want you to know there's another way to live. That there are people out there who will love and protect you. People who, if you let them into your life, will shower you—not with hurtful words but with words of kindness. With unconditional love.

Mother trauma goes deep, and I don't know if it ever really goes away. But it gets better. It did for me. Let me tell you about it—about my life then, with Jennie, and now.

CHAPTER 1

Mommy

COUSIN TREVOR IS HERE TODAY, AND HE'S SITTING ON the couch with Mommy. They're laughing and talking like nothing just happened. Like she hasn't been screaming at me and I haven't been crying. Like I didn't just tell her I'm running away.

I'm hiding behind the couch, quiet as a mouse. This is where I go sometimes to get away from the screaming. I wrap my arms around my legs and pull my knees up to my chin. It's dark here, but it feels safer than out there. Maybe I'll run away later, but for now, I'll just stay here and listen.

They must know I'm here behind the couch, that I can hear them talking.

"I wish she *would* run away," she says. Cousin laughs.

"Run far away and never come back."

Fresh tears spring from my eyes. She always tells me I should run away. This is the first time she's told someone else. It hurts more, for some reason, hearing her tell Cousin Trevor. It hurts in a different way—like it's real. Like she really means it.

I hug my knees tighter and bury my face in them to stifle my sobs. Quiet as a mouse.

Why does she want me to run away and never come back? I don't really want to go. I just say that. I want her to tell me to stay. I want her to love me.

She's my mommy.

They talk for a long time. I stay behind the couch. I won't run away this time. Maybe she'll change her mind. Maybe she'll come to me, take my hand, and pull me out from behind the couch. She'll hug me and say, "I'm sorry I screamed. I love you. Let's fix this. Let's be happy together."

Being happy is hard. In my house, the screaming is constant. It fills the whole house. Her voice rings in my brain like a siren going on and off all day. I try to be quiet and do the right things so I don't set off that alarm. But I don't know what the right things are.

It's the same for my brothers. They don't know how to be right either. We all get the screaming and the yelling and the ugly words. Her face turns red and she waves her arms. She's so angry and it's so scary. We don't even know why she's angry, and none of it makes sense. I want to know why. I want it to make sense. I want to fix it.

Sometimes we get soap in the mouth. Sometimes we get slaps in the face. Almost every day, we get the spankings. If we just knew how to be right for her, we could change. But we don't know. She won't tell us. So we run. We hide. We go outside where it's quiet and there is no yelling.

I like to go across the street to the churchyard. There's a big grassy field that people park their cars on when the parking lot's full. Most days, the field is empty, and I can hide in the grass and the bushes. I take branches and leaves and twigs and rocks and make a little home for myself there. There's a ditch, too, and I pretend that's my bathroom. This is my little safe place.

Sometimes my brothers are already in the field and I just go and find them, and sometimes they find me. Philip is one year older than me, and Andrew is three years older than me. We like this quiet place where we can laugh and play and there's no screaming. It's light here. In the house, it's dark and heavy. It's scary. It's loud.

We spend a lot of time in the field. Some days we just come home for lunch and dinner.

I wait behind the couch for a long time, until Cousin leaves. It seems like forever, but I don't want them to see me and my wet face. I want to be strong like Philip. He wouldn't cry.

Mommy doesn't get me from behind the couch. She's on the phone now talking to somebody else. I guess she forgot about me.

I'm four years old.

* * *

I don't run away this time. Daddy will be home soon, so I go to my room and wait. I wonder if today is a spanking day. I think it is. Mommy said to Philip this morning, "I'm going to tell your father when he gets home." So probably spankings.

I hear his truck. Daddy's home. He's been gone all day since before I woke up. He works two jobs sometimes. He's a mechanic for the County. Daddy looks tired. He's in his dirty work clothes. Mommy's yelling, telling him that we were bad today and we all need spankings. We're bad every day, and most days we get the spankings.

Me and Andrew and Philip go out back and line up against the shed. I'm first. Daddy asks me what I did today to get in trouble.

"Why are you in trouble, Miss?" he says. He always calls me

Miss, never Emily. Not sternly, though. That's just what Daddy calls me. What he's always called me.

I shake my head and tell him I don't remember. Then Daddy asks me if I want the hand, the paddle, or the belt, and I say, "the hand." I always say the hand because it doesn't hurt so much.

He spanks me, but it's not too bad. Some days the spankings really hurt, and some days Daddy pretends to spank us but doesn't. Like this time when he just pats me on the bum. I cry every time because I don't want Mommy to think I didn't get enough spankings. I'm crying now.

Next it's Philip's turn. Daddy talks to him about why he was bad today and same thing, the hand, the paddle, or the belt. Philip chooses the belt. He never picks the hand. I don't know why he always says "paddle" or "belt" because those hurt so much. No matter how many spankings Philip gets, he never cries.

It's Andrew's turn, and he's probably been the most bad. This morning when Mommy yelled at me and Philip, Andrew got in front of us and yelled back at her, and me and Philip ran away. Andrew tries to protect us, and I love him so much. When he yells at Mommy, we can get away. I love Philip too. They're my brothers.

Daddy talks to Andrew, and he gets the spankings, too, but not as many as Philip because Mommy said that Philip needed more. That doesn't make sense to me. Andrew was the baddest, so why does Philip get more spankings?

We get the spankings most days, usually when Daddy gets home, and first thing in the morning on Sundays, before church. Sometimes we get them later at night. It just depends.

I'm happy when Daddy comes homes. Even though he does

the spankings, it's always quieter in the house when he's home. He's calm like Mommy's daddy, my Pop-pop.

After spankings, Daddy takes a shower. He doesn't have to go to his other job tonight, so maybe after dinner we can play cards or Pictionary. We can be a family. A safe, happy family.

Tonight it's dinner and cards. It's quiet and nice. I wish Mommy could be quiet like this all the time. I wish she liked us.

* * *

I did something bad. I know because I got the slap and it hurts. Stings like a bee bit my cheek. I'm in the bathroom with Mommy, and she's yelling. Looking in the mirror. Looking at me. And yelling.

"I wasn't fat before I had you kids! It's your fault that I look like this."

It's my fault again. I made her fat. She grabs a bar of soap from the sink—uh oh, the soap. It's just a small bar, almost all used up. She puts it back on the sink and tells me to stand there and wait.

"Don't you move." I don't move, not a muscle. I stand still and quiet, quiet as a mouse.

She's in the kitchen now, opening cupboards and slamming them shut. Looking for something. Here she is with a bright green bottle. Dish soap.

"Open your mouth and stick out your tongue."

I do it. I have to. The soap hits my tongue, pools there, coats it. I start to gag and quickly cover my mouth with my hands. Hold it in until she says.

I must have done something really awful to get slapped and get soap. I'll probably get spankings when Daddy comes home, real ones this time. Mommy will tell him I need a lot of spankings today.

After a while, Mommy tells me to rinse my mouth and get out of the house and don't come back until dinner.

I rinse and spit, rinse and spit. Then I run. I'm crying and running, crying and running. Running into the field.

* * *

Daddy sold our tiny house. He says we're getting a big new house, but it isn't built yet. So for now, we're staying with Grandma and Pop-pop. Some days it's nice because I get to see my Pop-pop. Not every day is nice though.

Today was loud. Grandma and Mommy have been yelling all day. At least they haven't been yelling at me so much. I think they're angry at each other. It's dark out and we should all be in bed, but I think Mommy forgot about us with all the yelling.

Now Mommy yells at us, "Get in the car!" Me and my brothers get in the car. We're not in trouble, I don't think. Maybe Mommy just wants to get away from Grandma.

Daddy pulls up in his truck. He worked both jobs today, so he's home really late.

Mommy's backing out of the driveway with all us kids in the car, and Daddy's waving at her to stop. "Where are you going?" he says, "Come back inside!"

But she's still backing up, so Daddy opens the car door and jumps in. Mommy drives away, still yelling and screaming. She's driving kind of crazy and it's a jerky, bumpy ride. Daddy's talking to her in a nice voice, but she's still yelling.

We stop on a bridge and Mommy jumps out, the car still running. She's gone in the dark. *Where is she?*

Me and my brothers are all crying now, calling for Mommy.

Daddy looks at us in the back seat and says it's going to be okay. We just have to wait.

We sit there in the car for a long time. My face is all sticky from crying, and I'm so tired. I want Mommy to come back. I want to go home to my bed and go to sleep. I'm so tired.

She comes back and gets in the car, this time on the passenger side. Daddy drives us home and puts us to bed. I'm worried about more yelling, but Grandma's in her bedroom, so we can all go to sleep now. I hope everyone stays asleep, especially Mommy and Grandma.

* * *

Pop-pop and Grandma are both home today. Mommy and Grandma are yelling at each other like they usually do, so Pop-pop takes me and my brothers outside to do yard work. We climb the orange trees and pick fruit. I can hear the yelling out here, but at least no one's yelling at me. I love my Pop-pop. He makes me feel safe so I don't have to hide. I wish he would stay every day.

Most days, like today, I go back to the field. I spend hours here. I come to the field after breakfast and go home for lunch, then I come back again until dinner, then back again until bedtime. I come here when Mommy locks me out of the house, but mostly I come here because I want to. There's no screaming in the field.

In the tall grass I wipe my face with my hands, then I wipe my hands on my pants. Make the tears go away. I peek between the privacy hedges, looking for Andrew and Philip, but they're not here. I'm alone in the field today. That's okay, I'm alone a lot of the time. The other little kids on the street don't come into the field. I guess they stay home or they play in their yards.

I don't know. But I don't think I'm the only four-year-old on the street. There are other houses, and sometimes I see people coming in and out of them. I don't know where other little girls go when they run away.

The church parking lot is empty, and I have the whole field to play in. I just ate lunch, and I don't know when dinnertime is in the house, so I'll just play until I'm hungry again.

I gather branches and vines and leaves and make a pile. This will be my kitchen. I lay the branches on the ground in a big square—my kitchen table. Then I sit in the grass and weave some of the smaller branches and vines into a little chair seat. I put rocks on the table for my cup and plate, and I add two more place settings in case Andrew and Philip show up.

After dinner in the field, I go down to the ditch to wash my little stone dishes. This is where I would take a bath, too, if this was my house. My safe little house. But no bath tonight. It's getting later, but I'm not hungry yet, and I'm not sure if it's dinnertime in the real house. I'll go back to my house in the field and see if Andrew or Philip are there. I can ask them if it's time to go home.

No Andrew and no Philip. I don't know what to do. I spread the rest of the dry grass and leaves on the ground and pat them into a little bed. I make a pillow too.

I lie on my grassy bed and stare at the sky. So calm. So quiet. I close my eyes.

"Emily, it's time for dinner." It's Philip. He's shaking my shoulder, gently. I must have fallen asleep.

I stand up and my back feels cold and wet. Sweaty. Philip helps me brush the grass and leaves from my legs and back. He takes my hand. The streetlights come on as we cross the field toward home.

* * *

We moved into the new house and it's bigger. I'm getting bigger too.

My hair is getting so long. It's blond and curly, and sometimes Mommy puts it in pigtails. Other times, she makes it a ponytail and adds a bow. It's so long I can chew on it, and I do. I have to be careful though because if Mommy sees me, she yells.

"Get your hair out of your mouth!" she says, "If you don't stop chewing on it, I'm going to cut it all off!"

I must have been chewing on my hair just now, because she's yelling. I don't even remember putting it in my mouth, but there it is, the end of my ponytail, all wet.

'That's it," she says. "It's all coming off!" Mommy's holding the kitchen shears in her hand. She grabs my arm and pulls me behind her to the garage. She plunks me onto a stool and starts chopping. My curls fall onto my lap, onto the cement floor.

I'm crying, sobbing, "No, no, no, Mommy, please don't cut my hair!"

"If you would have listened to me, then I wouldn't have to do this," she says.

Andrew must have heard my cries. He comes into the garage and he has this look on his face like he can't believe what he's seeing.

"*What are you doing?*" he says.

Mommy stops cutting and says, "Well, I told her to stop chewing on her hair and she didn't, so I'm cutting all her hair off." Andrew goes back into the house.

I hop off the stool and run into the house, into the bathroom. I look in the mirror. My hair is all choppy. It's a mess. I don't even want to look at it. I cover my face with my hands and sob.

Mommy comes into the bathroom and stands behind me.

"I guess now I'm going to have to take you to the barbershop to fix this. Just one more thing I didn't need!"

She's so angry, and it's all my fault. I don't know why but it is.

I go to bed with my messed-up hair.

* * *

Me, Philip, Andrew, and Mommy are all going to the barbershop. My brothers are laughing at me and my stupid hair. I'm really upset, and that makes them laugh even more. Mommy's still mad.

"If you would have just listened to me and stopped chewing on your hair, we wouldn't even be going to the barbershop. Stop your crying, Emily. I don't want to hear any more crying out of you today."

I sit in the big chair and the barber starts cutting. My hair's already so short; all he can do is give me a boy's cut. All my curls are gone now—every last one. I'm crying my eyes out. *Why did this happen?*

"I look like a boy now!" I holler.

My brothers laugh and laugh. Mommy doesn't say anything.

For a while, people say how me and Andrew look just like twins. Even people who don't know us say that. People on the street. I hang my head down and cry. But I will never chew on my hair again.

* * *

I don't think Mommy likes me and my brothers very much, but she likes animals. If there's a turtle crossing the road, she stops the car to save it. If she sees a stray dog, she brings it home. If Philip and Andrew find a snake in the backyard, as long as it's not poisonous, they get to keep it as a pet. Sometimes we have bunnies and lizards, and we even had a squirrel, a raccoon, and an injured dove. For a while, we had a little pony until my parents found a new home for it.

The best pet is Philip's new English bulldog puppy, Elmer Fudd. Philip loves that little dog.

Elmer Fudd keeps growing and growing until he's bigger than a puppy. Mommy says he's "rambunctious." I think that means he jumps around a lot.

Today's Sunday, and we're coming home from church. I walk in the door, and here comes Elmer Fudd, just like always, to greet us. He runs right into me and knocks me over. I'm a little surprised, and I start to cry. I'm okay though, not hurt.

Mommy's yelling. "That's it," she hollers, "We're getting rid of that dog!"

They take Elmer Fudd away, and we never see him again. It's like that with all the pets. They stay awhile, then Mommy gets rid of them. Pets don't behave, just like me and my brothers don't behave. We all make Mommy mad.

* * *

My bedroom is in the front part of the house, and it has a big window. Mommy calls it a bay window. Tonight I'm in bed sleeping, or trying to go to sleep, but there's a face in that window. Someone's looking at me. I tell my parents and Mommy says, "You're making things up, Emily. Go back to bed."

So I do. I see the face again a few nights later, and again I tell my parents, "Someone's watching me." It happens again and again, but no one will believe me. I'm scared at night, scared of that little person in the window. *Who is he? What does he want? What if he comes in?*

This morning Daddy went outside to look at my window. He saw handprints.

It's nighttime and Daddy's hiding in my bedroom. He wants to see for himself. Sure enough, here comes that little person peeking in my window. Daddy runs outside and chases after him, yelling his head off.

"Get off our property! I'm calling the police!"

I feel better now, safer. Daddy puts a trellis outside my window with a vine growing on it so no one can look in my window again. But I never go near dark windows anymore. I always want the blinds closed when it gets dark.

*　*　*

Daddy and Mommy sold our big house and bought Grandma and Pop-pop's house, so we live here now. Grandma and Pop-pop moved into another house a little further away. I want Mommy to be happy in this house, but today she's not happy at all.

"Come here, Emily," she says, "I want to show you something." We're in the kitchen and she takes an old coffee can down from a cabinet shelf and opens it. It's full of dollar bills.

"Look at this," she shrieks, "This is all the money your father gives me for groceries for you kids for three whole weeks!"

She counts it out and lays the bills on the kitchen table. "One hundred and ten dollars! For five people! It's not enough. I don't know what he expects me to do with this."

My mother keeps talking, saying bad things about my daddy. I wonder, *Are we poor?* That doesn't make sense because Daddy works two jobs. He's hardly ever home. We have food to eat and clothes to wear, and toys just like all the other kids. Maybe just my mother is poor and that's why she's so mad. But she goes to the beauty salon and gets her hair done whenever she wants. She gets her nails done every week. She has a checkbook, and I've seen her use it at the grocery store. But my mother wouldn't lie. I don't understand.

* * *

Philip started school this year. I see him go in the morning and Andrew too. I want to go with them. Mommy does the dishes, then she sits in the big brown chair in the living room. I crawl onto her lap and she rocks me back and forth.

"I want to go to school like Andrew and Philip."

"No, Emily, it's just you and me here now."

"I could go to preschool. I'm big enough. Some of the other kids on the street are going this year and they're four too."

"No, this is my job. You stay home with me, and I take care of you."

I don't want her to take care of me. I want to go to school.

Being at home alone with Mommy scares me. Daddy's at work all day and now Andrew and Philip are gone. There's no one to protect me. I must be very quiet and not disturb Mommy. I don't know what she'll do.

Most days I play in the closet. I keep my bedroom dark and turn on the closet light, go inside, and close the door. I make up songs and dances. I don't go to the field as much because my brothers are gone and I don't want to be alone, but I'm afraid to be around Mommy all by myself. She never comes to the closet.

CHAPTER 2

Mother

IT'S SUNDAY, MY FAVORITE DAY OF THE WEEK. DADDY doesn't work on Sundays, and we're all out of school for the summer. No work, no school, and no homework. Today we get to be a family.

I can't believe I'm finally in the double digits—ten years old! Just one more year of elementary school, then I get to go to middle school with Philip. I'm so excited. Maybe I'll make some new friends. But today it's all about Daddy, Andrew, Philip, and my mother. And me, Emily.

It's going to be a good day; I can just tell. First of all, there are no spankings today. I don't know why, but my mother doesn't even mention it. Second, it's Sunday. Daddy's at work all the other days and we hardly ever see him. This is the day he spends with us and it's always a wonderful quiet day.

Today we go to church, then we all go out to lunch. On the drive home, Daddy asks who's up for a game of baseball. All of us! We all want to play! Daddy could suggest anything and we'd say yes. He's the best daddy in the world and when he's home, I'm happy. I think Andrew and Philip are happy too. I don't know if my mother's happy, but she's a lot quieter.

After baseball in the front yard, we change into our swimsuits and head into the backyard and the swimming pool. We play games, then I just lie back in the water and float. It's so peaceful, lying here in the pool, staring at the sky. I close my eyes for a moment and am overcome with sadness. Tears stream from my eyes. I don't know why. I wipe them away. I look across the pool at Daddy, and Andrew, and Philip. They're playing a game in the water, laughing and splashing around. I shouldn't be sad.

I close my eyes again. A memory. I'm four years old, lying in the field. In my little grass bed. The sun's warm and there's a gentle breeze. Calm.

"Emily, time for dinner." Philip's shaking my shoulder, gently. He asks, "Are you okay?"

"Yeah," I say, wiping the tears with my fingertips. I smile at Philip. "I'm okay." Because I am, in this moment, just fine.

* * *

We moved again. I don't know why we move so much, but at least this time we didn't go far. We're right next door. It's a nice house, but there's no pool like our old house.

Even though I'm older now, I still see Pop-pop a lot. Every Tuesday, we volunteer together at the soup kitchen next to the church. Today my friend Sheri is with us, and we're getting everything ready before the people show up to eat.

The soup kitchen is a big room with long tables and metal chairs in the middle where the people sit, and buffet tables on two sides. One side is for hot food, and the other side is for cold food and utensils. Behind the hot food tables is a swinging door that opens to the kitchen. The adults are in there cooking and filling up the hot pans for the buffet line. There's another swinging door on the opposite side of the room that opens to a storage area and the bathrooms.

All the people are waiting outside, but it's not time. This one guy, Marvin, has to use the bathroom, so they let him in early. He heads through the swinging door behind my table, but I don't really pay much attention because there's a lot to do. I just get back to work.

This is only Sheri's second time at the soup kitchen, and I can tell she likes it. It's fun to pretend we work in a real restaurant, plus, we're helping people. We put the salad in bowls and pour juice into cups. We set out the bread and make sure all the napkins, knives, forks, and spoons are stacked neatly for our guests. It's almost time to open the doors, so we take a little bathroom break. The men's and ladies' bathrooms are in a hallway behind the storage area. They face each other, boys on the left and girls on the right. We're in the ladies' room talking away. It's nice to have a friend here with me today. I love working at the soup kitchen, and it's even better with Sheri.

We wash our hands, just like always, and head to our stations. But when we open the bathroom door to leave, Marvin is standing there in front of the men's room. He's holding his penis, and I can't even look because I know what he's doing, and it's not something I want to see. I'm standing here in shock and so is Sheri, and Marvin's talking to us, and now he's coming toward us. He's after us, and he's still doing that thing. We look around for help, but there's no one back here. All the adults are up front in the kitchen. Marvin's trying to block us, and I feel trapped, but me and Sheri get around him somehow and we go around a table so it's between him and us, and then we make a run for the door.

They're opening the doors to the soup kitchen, and we go to our stations. We don't say anything to the adults. We just serve everybody like nothing happened, like we didn't just see some guy masturbating right in front of us and he didn't just chase us around the back of the soup kitchen.

Marvin's in line and we serve him too. He doesn't say anything, and I can't believe he's behaving like nothing happened, but I don't want to look at him, and I don't want him to look at me. I don't want to think about it at all.

"We can't tell anyone," I say to Sheri. "No one can know." I don't know why I say this, but I don't want to have to talk about it to anyone. This is a bad thing that happened to us, and I don't want anyone to know. I mean, we didn't do anything wrong. We're just eleven. But it's bad, and I don't want to get in trouble.

Marvin eats his meal and leaves. It's over, and I don't want to think about it ever again.

* * *

On the ride home, I don't tell my Pop-pop what happened, and I don't say anything to my parents about it. I'm worried about Sheri though because I think her family would talk about something like this. I think they'd do something about it. Sheri wouldn't get in trouble.

I'm in bed thinking about all this and trying to get to sleep. It's late, and the phone rings in the kitchen. I can hear my mother's voice. She must be talking to someone on the phone, but I can't hear what she's saying. Now she's talking to my daddy. Oh no, I bet it's about what happened today. And I'm in trouble. I'm scared, lying here. I can't make out what they're saying, just murmurs. Now footsteps.

I sleep with my door cracked open. From my daybed, which

is pushed up against the wall, I can see the light from the kitchen. The door is pushed open, lighting up a whole wall in my room. They're standing in the doorway, in silhouette against the kitchen light. They don't turn my light on or even come in, probably because my brothers' room is next to mine and they don't want to wake them up.

"Emily, come out to the kitchen. We want to talk to you about what happened today." My mother's voice sounds different. Concerned. I get up and follow them into the kitchen. We sit around the table.

My daddy looks sad and angry at the same time, but he doesn't say anything. My mother says, "Sheri's mother just called. Tell us what happened today at the soup kitchen."

I'm so nervous. I don't want to make her mad. I don't want to get yelled at. I press my hands together and squeeze them between my knees under the table. That steadies me, keeps me from shaking. Then I tell them what happened.

It seems like they just want to make sure the story is true. They ask me a few questions, but they don't push for a lot of details. I'm grateful for that because I don't want to talk about it at all. I can tell Daddy's getting angrier because he's tapping his fingers on the table. I guess that steadies him, just like pressing my hands between my knees does for me. His tone is soft though. His anger isn't for me; it's for the man at the soup kitchen. Marvin.

My mother's tone is soft, too, which is weird. They tell me to go back to bed, and they'll take care of it in the morning.

There's no yelling, no blaming, no shame. Maybe I'm not in trouble after all.

* * *

I see Sheri at school and I'm afraid to talk to her. It's just awkward, I guess, and will be for a while. I'm embarrassed and ashamed that this happened to me, happened to us. Even though my mother didn't blame me, I still feel like it's my fault. Seeing Sheri makes it worse because she was there. She knows. It's like we both did something very wrong together, and even if I never talk about it again, she'll always know. She saw. I tell myself I did nothing wrong, so why do I feel like this? I don't know.

In middle school, we change classes a lot, and Sheri's not in many of mine, so it's pretty easy to avoid her. I'm glad she told, even though I asked her not to. My parents said they'll take care of it. Maybe that will make all of this go away.

* * *

After dinner, Daddy shoos Andrew and Philip into the living room to watch TV. I'm in my pajamas, getting ready for bed, when the sheriff comes by. He's a detective, and I know him because he's one of my brother Philip's best friend's stepdad. Philip's been to his house, and I know I can trust him. I feel safe with him here.

Sheriff Detective Parker says he has some photographs for me to look at, a "photo lineup" he calls it. My mother and me and the detective sit at the kitchen table. Daddy goes into the living room.

The sheriff lays out six pictures on the kitchen table in two rows—three on top and three on the bottom.

"Is the man who did this in any of these pictures?"

I point to the middle photograph in the bottom row, but I don't say a word.

The sheriff shakes his head. "Thank you," he says. "You did a great job."

Then he says that I didn't do anything wrong and that he's going to take care of it. I'm still embarrassed and ashamed, but hearing someone say that I didn't do anything wrong makes me feel a little better.

* * *

It's Saturday and I'm at the sheriff's office with my mother. The sheriff wants to talk to me about what happened, the "incident." I'm a little nervous because I haven't talked about it to anyone but my parents, that night in the kitchen. My mother checks in at the front desk, and we sit in the plastic chairs in the waiting room. After a few minutes, Sheriff Parker comes out of a door and stands in the lobby. He tells us to come with him. He takes us to an interview room in the back of the station. Another detective is there who I don't know, and Sheriff Parker introduces us.

Me and my mother sit on one side of the table, and the two detectives sit on the other side. There's a photo lineup on the table, and the sheriff asks me to point to the man who exposed himself at the soup kitchen. I don't know if it's the same lineup he showed me the other night or a new one, but I recognize Marvin immediately. I tap the photo.

"Before we get started, can I get you anything? A soda?" he asks. I nod my head. He leaves the room and comes back with a can of soda. This is a real treat because I never get soda at home. My mother doesn't say anything, so I guess she approves.

Then the sheriff says he wants me to tell him and the other detective what happened that day.

"Tell us exactly what happened from start to finish, and don't leave out any details," he says.

I'm glad the sheriff is here. His voice is kind, and having him here instead of just the new detective makes me less nervous.

I tell my story. The detectives ask me a few questions, but mostly they just let me talk. They want to know where me and Sheri were and what we were doing. They want to know where everyone else in the soup kitchen was. And they want to know about Marvin.

For once, I'm glad my father isn't here beside me. I usually look to Daddy for support, but I think hearing this again would just make him uncomfortable. And really angry—not at me, but at Marvin. I remember him tapping his fingers on the kitchen table, the look on his face. This would be hard for Daddy.

It takes a couple of hours to tell the whole thing and answer all their questions, but I'm finally done.

"That's great," says the sheriff, "You did wonderful, Emily."

The other detective tells me that I did nothing wrong, and even though Sheriff Parker said that the other night, it's nice hearing it again. They thank me for my help and tell my mother and me not to worry about anything because they're going to take care of it.

"What about court?" my mother wants to know. "Since Emily is a witness, is she going to have to do that?"

I can tell she's worried about this. I hadn't even thought of it.

The sheriff says that if the case goes to trial, I would have to testify. I do not want to see Marvin again, and I really don't want to tell my story to a bunch of strangers.

"We're hoping to avoid that though. With the evidence and the testimonies of both girls, we may have enough on this guy to just lock him up."

Then he says he'll let us know if he needs to talk to us again, and we leave.

The drive home is short and quiet. My mother doesn't say anything, and I'm glad about that. I'm not in trouble.

She never mentions it again. But my daddy says I can't go to the soup kitchen anymore.

* * *

My brothers don't ask me about what happened. We don't talk about things like that in our family. Philip probably knows more than I do about the case from talking to his friend whose stepdad is Detective Parker, the guy who's working on the case. Maybe he's telling our big brother, Andrew, about it. I don't know. I'm just glad they don't ask me anything because it's embarrassing.

* * *

It's different in the house now. My mother is quiet. She doesn't yell. She doesn't make me feel like it was a burden for her to deal with all of this—having the sheriff come to our house, taking me to the station to speak with the detectives and do that second photo lineup. For the first time, I don't feel like I'm making her life harder. I feel protected.

I'm not in trouble, and I think maybe my mother cares about me. I hope it stays like this.

* * *

My brothers don't say anything to me about what happened until a few days later when Marvin's arrested.

"Hey Emily," Philip says, "They arrested that guy who did that thing to you and Sheri."

My brothers update me every time there's a story. My name isn't in the paper because I'm a minor, but there's a mugshot of Marvin.

Deep shame. Embarrassment. I don't want my brothers talking about it, knowing about it. I shouldn't feel this way; I didn't do anything wrong. The detectives said so. But still, I feel responsible. Like I could have prevented it. Like I brought it on myself.

There's no trial. He's sentenced to two years in jail plus probation. I find out about all this from Andrew and Philip.

After that, there's no more volunteering at the soup kitchen for me, and no one ever mentions it again. Everything goes back to the way it was before. The way it's been as far back as I can remember. My mother goes back to being my mother—Mommy.

* * *

My mother's parents, Grandma and Pop-pop, live out west of town on an acre of land. There's a pond near their house, and when we were younger, me, Andrew, and Philip used to splash in it and try to catch frogs. Those were fun times.

In the summers, we stay with them at least one weekend every month. Grandma and Pop-pop take us with them to Lexington, Kentucky. One summer, I got to go to Maine, just me and Grandma and Pop-pop, for six weeks. Andrew got to go to Las Vegas, and Philip went to Niagara Falls.

Pop-pop loves all of his grandkids. Sometimes me and my brothers go to our grandparents' house together, but other times we each get to go alone. Me and Pop-pop have a special connection. Sometimes I call him and say, "I don't feel good today. Can you come get me?" And he always does.

Their house is always clean, spotless. Grandma has a cabinet with glass doors where she keeps her figurines. We aren't allowed to touch them. She likes to read books and play solitaire, and sometimes one of her friends comes over to play gin rummy. Grandma lets me watch, but I can never play with them.

Sometimes me and Pop-pop play cards in the house too. He teaches me to play blackjack. Mostly we play outside. He pushes me on the tire swing and lets me ride the lawn mower around the yard. He takes me with him to do work in the yard and keep the plants looking nice. There's a banana tree in the backyard, and he holds me up so I can check the bananas to see if they're ready to be picked. We drive around and look for cans to take to the recycling center. First, we pop all the tabs off the tops. Then we use the smasher to crush the cans. When we have enough, we take them to the recycling center and get money for them. One time, we used the money to pay to pick strawberries. Another time, we got ice cream.

Being around my Pop-pop is comforting. He listens to me and has conversations with me like I'm an adult. He always makes me feel safe and loved. I call him the love of my life, and he calls me that too. I'll never love anyone the way I love Pop-pop. I love Daddy, too, but it's different.

* * *

My mother keeps the house spick-and-span just like the old house. She's always cleaning. I swear she mops the floors every day, and God forbid if we step foot on a wet floor. We get yelled at if we mess anything up.

My mother hasn't been yelling as much lately though.

Maybe she likes this house better? I don't know. She's been spending a lot of time on the phone talking to her friends. She's always talked on the phone a lot, but now she does it even more.

Daddy bought a computer, and she's on that a lot too. We just got the internet, and I'm not sure what it is exactly, but there's something called a modem that makes a loud screeching noise when my mother starts it up, then it's quiet for a long time. The computer's in the den, and my mother closes the sliding door so we can't hear her or see her, but I don't mind. It's nice. She never talks about what she does for hours on that computer, and I never ask her. I don't care. I'm not even curious. All I know is that she isn't paying attention to me and I can be in the house and not get yelled at.

* * *

My mother has been so different lately. I don't know why, but I like it. She's even been happy. And not just for one day or part of a day. It's been a few weeks. She's feeling good and not yelling at us. We don't get in trouble every day.

She asks, "How was school today?"

"Ummm...fine."

She wants to help us with our homework. This is weird. She never does that. We don't know what's the matter. We still walk on our tiptoes and try to be quiet and good. We don't want it to change.

* * *

Mommy came home with a brace on her leg. It looks like jelly inside plastic. She's in the kitchen telling Daddy that she went to the doctor and he gave her a new prescription for her pain.

Mommy's always walked with a limp, and her one ankle has never looked like the other one. It's because of an accident she had a long time ago. She's told us the story many times, and I think about it now.

When she was a teenager, she told me and my brothers, she was riding a horse and it got spooked. They were headed straight toward a ditch, so she jumped off. My mother landed hard. She broke both of her legs, messed up her knees and hips, and shattered her ankle. They had to put pins and screws in her bones where her left ankle was supposed to be. It still hurts her to walk.

Maybe these new pills will help. I go into the bathroom and peek in the medicine cabinet. There's a new bottle with the word *OxyContin* printed on the label.

It must be helping because my mother doesn't just stay home anymore. She goes to the gym every day. Sometimes she's gone for hours.

* * *

I like being a teenager, and I really like middle school. I'm out of the house all day five days a week, and after school, I drop my books off at home and walk across the street to the church. They have an after-school program for younger kids, and I'm a volunteer. Philip and Andrew have sports practice after school, and I have the church.

We don't get spankings anymore, so we don't have to be home when Daddy gets home. Instead, we just get grounded or we have things taken away, like maybe no bike riding for a week or something. Our mother still tells Daddy what we did wrong and he doles out the punishments. I still get yelled at, but lately it seems that Philip and Daddy are mostly in trouble.

I don't know what they're doing wrong, but our mother seems like she's angry at them a lot.

* * *

It's not so bad lately. Things seem more predictable, more... settled. We help our mother a lot with the laundry and the housework. We clean our own bedrooms and take turns cleaning the bathroom. With our daily chores, plus school, plus my volunteer work and my brothers in sports, we've fallen into a kind of rhythm. Our mother goes to the gym every day, and we all have dinner together at night. The routine is nice.

I'm lying in bed, thinking about all this, wondering what's changed. It seems like our mother's changed. When did she change? I think it was after she went to the doctor. Maybe when we got the computer and she started going to the gym. I don't know for sure, but there's not as much screaming as there used to be.

I hear my mother now in the living room, talking to Daddy, and now yelling. *Why is she yelling?* He's yelling back too. This isn't right—it's been so quiet, and my mother and Daddy never fight, at least not where I can see them or hear them. They do it in private, quietly, and away from us kids. But right now they're so loud! They must know I can hear them.

My daddy's voice: "Just come to bed, Jennie, and we'll talk about it tomorrow." My mother yells some more, then it's quiet again.

* * *

It's been a few days since the big fight. Nobody said anything about it and I didn't ask. I don't want to know. I'm coming up to the house after school, and I just want to dump my backpack so I can go across the street for my volunteer work with the kids. My mother's outside. *What is she doing?*

She's loading up the van, our bright blue Astro van. Daddy and Philip are playing basketball in the driveway. They're not helping. What's going on?

"Where are you going?" I ask.

My mother says, "I'm going away for a couple of weeks. I'll be staying with your aunts in Maryland, and I'll be back in two weeks. I just need to take a vacation for a while."

"Okay," I say. I go into the house and put my backpack in my room, then I come back outside and say goodbye. There's no hugging or anything, but I guess that's normal. My mother stopped hugging me when I was little.

I go across the street to the church to do my volunteer work. One of the teachers, Alyssa, is there. She asks, "Is something wrong, Emily?"

"No," I say. But something is wrong. My mother doesn't take vacations by herself. This is weird. I push it out of my mind and get to work.

* * *

It's late when the last kids are picked up from the church and I can go home. In my bedroom, there's something on my bed. A pink razor! Oh my gosh, I've been begging for permission to shave my legs for years. I just asked last week, and my mother said no. I guess it must be okay now.

I carry the razor into the living room, but no one's there. Should I ask Daddy about it? No, this must be a present from my mother, and she's not here. Then I notice something. Things are missing. Not just the clothes and bathroom stuff that I would expect Mommy to take with her on vacation but other stuff. Her knickknacks are all gone. The little cow and the pig. All the little glass farm animals. Other things too. My mother took all of her stuff with her on vacation.

But I can shave my legs! I take the razor into the bathroom and look at it under the bright lights. It's a Venus with three blades. Disposable, which is just fine. I'm so nervous—I've never done this before. I put one leg up on the edge of the bathtub and scrape the razor across my skin. It kind of stings, but I keep going. I do the whole leg, then I do the other one. This hurts, but it must be right. I look at my legs in the mirror. No cuts, but they're a little sore.

Maybe tomorrow I'll shave my armpits.

* * *

I'm at my friend Sheri's house. It's not the same between us since the Marvin incident—we don't hang out like we used to. But today's her birthday and she invited me to the party, so here I am.

I can't believe Sheri got razors for her birthday.

"Yay!" I say, "I got a razor too!"

Sheri's mom asks me if I used it yet, and I tell her about how I shaved my legs and my armpits and how it stung a little.

"Oh, Emily," she says, "you shaved your legs dry? Didn't you put anything on them, like water at least?"

I shake my head. No one told me about the water.

"Next time get them wet first, with some water or soap, or your dad's shaving cream. Then it won't sting."

I feel a little silly, but she's so nice and I'm glad to learn about shaving my legs. I wonder what else I don't know, what my mother didn't tell me.

CHAPTER 3

Jennie

MY MOTHER JENNIE HAS BEEN GONE A MONTH. SCHOOL'S
out for the summer, and it's been really pleasant around here.
We all stick to our routines and our chores—laundry, housework—and Daddy has been trying to do all the other stuff that
our mother used to do. I help him out whenever I can. I don't
mind at all, especially since everything's so different. I'm not
walking on eggshells anymore. Andrew and Philip seem more
relaxed, too, and even Daddy is smiling a lot more. No more
explosions. No arguments.

It's Saturday morning, and Philip, Andrew, and I are watching cartoons on TV in the living room. Daddy comes in and sees
us. He gets upset. He doesn't yell, but he talks in a serious voice.

"Why aren't you doing your chores?"

"It's early. We'll do them after this show."

We're not trying to talk back. There's lots of time to do
chores. Cartoons are only on for another half an hour.

"Kids," he says, "We're all going to have to start doing even
more around the house because your mom's not coming back."

We all look at Daddy. He can't be serious.

"But she *said* she's coming back!" I insist.

Daddy shakes his head. His eyes are red and watery. *Was Daddy crying?*

"No, Miss," he says again, "she's not coming back."

I get up and go into the bathroom so they can't see me cry. It's my turn to clean the bathroom anyway. I pour the cleaner in the toilet and sit on the tub. My tears drip off my face and make wet spots on my pants.

What does he mean, she's not coming back? She told me she was coming back. *Why would she lie to me? How can our mother just leave? Leave her family?*

* * *

I'm staying with Grandma and Pop-pop for a weekend. My brothers didn't want to come this time—they don't think it's cool to hang out with the grandparents anymore. I guess I'm not cool yet. Maybe in one or two years I'll be cool like Philip and Andrew, but this weekend, I'd rather be with Grandma and Pop-pop.

Grandma makes me lunch, a tuna sandwich with Lay's potato chips. I'm sitting at the glass table with metal legs, and I have my chair pushed back while I eat my sandwich. Grandma walks up and pinches my belly.

"You're getting fat," she says. "When you're done eating that meal I prepared for you, you should do some sit-ups."

I don't want to hear that. I already feel weird and awkward in my body, wearing a bra and shaving my legs.

I feel bad, and I want Grandma to like me and not tell me I'm fat. On Sunday afternoon, she's watching TV in the sun-room, the Florida room, with Pop-pop. I sit on the couch to keep her company. Maybe she'll talk with me like Pop-pop does.

When it's a commercial, Grandma looks at me and says, "You know it's your fault that your mother left, and it's your fault she's not coming back. You and your brothers. If the three of you had been better, she never would have left."

I don't say anything. I can't. Maybe if I don't react, don't even move a muscle, she won't say anything else. I already know it's my fault, but that doesn't mean I want to talk about it.

She keeps talking. "If you had called her after she left, she would have come back."

How was I supposed to call her? I don't know where she is, I think, but don't say out loud. I'm feeling ashamed but angry too. *Why is this my responsibility? I'm just a kid!*

I'm sad all the time because my mother is gone. Grandma just made me feel even sadder. I can't cry though, not in front of my grandma, even though my feelings are so hurt. I think that would make it worse.

Pop-pop is quiet. Grandma likes to yell, just like my mother, and he doesn't want the yelling to start. Grandma wants to scream and argue. She wants a fight. Pop-pop wants to keep the peace.

Later, in the kitchen, he tells me, "It's going to be okay, Emily. You are my sweet girl."

Grandma walks in right then. She must have been listening just outside the doorway.

"Don't tell her she's sweet," she says. "She might actually believe it." She chuckles, and I can't tell if it's a teasing chuckle or a mean chuckle.

Pop-pop is sad, but he's mad too.

"Just go away," he tells Grandma. "Just stop."

* * *

I don't tell my friends what I'm going through. Everyone knows my mother is gone, but I don't talk about it. It seems like everyone is staring at me all the time anyway. I'm that girl with the messed-up family. I stop going to church as much. People are always talking about us. It's embarrassing.

I'm not friends with the kids I knew from elementary school, the ones with normal families and mothers that didn't run away and abandon them. They are all so happy—better than my family. Better than me. I feel ashamed when I see them out together with their families. I stop hanging out with them, and I find new friends. My best friend in middle school has a mom, a sister, and a stepdad. Her family's different, like mine. I feel better around people with different families. Less weird.

Then there's this girl Kim who lives down the street. She's really cool. And nice. We walk home from school together, and sometimes we go to the park and prank call people from the payphone.

Kim doesn't judge me. I can tell her anything and she gets it. She gets *me*.

* * *

Daddy works a lot to make money and take care of us. I don't always have the coolest clothes, but I have enough clothes, and they're always clean. Whenever I need new shoes, Daddy gives me money and lets me pick them out.

He gives Andrew his little gold truck, a Toyota pickup. He tells him, "Listen, now that you're driving, I'm giving you my truck. I have to work, so if your brother and sister need to go somewhere, I need you to take them."

Andrew huffs and puffs when we tell him we need to go

somewhere, but he takes us. The rest of the time, he's at his friends' houses.

Daddy gets a new car, an ugly gray one. We call it a *hooptie*. It's old and beat-up. The cloth hangs down from the roof in the back, and there's just one row of seats. It's embarrassing. I don't want to ride in it. The air conditioner doesn't even work, so we have to drive around with the windows down. *What if someone sees me in this terrible car?*

Andrew's never home, except to pick up clean clothes. Philip is around more. He has friends come over. When they start driving, he goes out with them. When he's old enough to drive, too, he gets a job as a busboy at a restaurant so he can buy his own car. When he's home, he sits in his room or watches TV. We're still kind of ghosts in the house, living our own lives. I guess I'm just used to it now.

* * *

School's out for the summer. Andrew comes into my room and says, "Hey, Grandma called. Mom's back in town. She's there, and they want us to come visit."

We set up a time to come over, in the afternoon on a day when Philip doesn't have to work. Andrew's girlfriend rides with him in the little gold truck, and I ride with Philip in his black Lumina.

It feels like we're just going to visit Grandma and Pop-pop, but inside I'm nervous. I think Philip is too. We haven't seen or spoken to our mother in over a year. That's a lot longer than the two weeks she said she'd be gone! I don't know what's going to happen. I don't even know what I *want* to happen.

Andrew gets there first, but he waits for us so we can all walk in together. He's so casual. "Hey, Grandma. Hey, Pop-pop."

I can see Jennie sitting there. She stands up when we walk in. She looks the same. Exactly the same.

"Hi, guys," she says. She runs up to us, puts her arms around first Andrew, then Philip, then me. None of us hug her back. I stand there with my arms by my side. This is so awkward.

Grandma says, "What do you guys want to eat?"

"We're not hungry," says Philip.

"I don't want anything to eat," I say.

We get sodas from the fridge and sit in the Florida room. I make sure to sit in a chair, so I don't have to sit on the couch next to my mom. Philip takes that seat. Andrew and his girlfriend sit across from them.

"How are you? How's school?" Mom asks.

Andrew's the only one who speaks. "It's fine," he snaps.

"I can't believe you're both driving!"

What is happening? Why is everyone sitting around talking like everything is normal? This isn't normal! That's what's in my head right now. I cannot believe this.

I guess Andrew can't believe it either because he says, "How can you sit here and just talk to us, acting like nothing even happened? Of course we're driving. You've been gone thirteen months! Why did you leave?"

She doesn't say anything, so he keeps yelling. "Why didn't you come back? Why didn't you call us?"

Grandma stands up and yells at Andrew. "Don't talk to your mother like that! She's here now. She loves you, and she wants to hear about your lives."

Jennie stands up too. "Why are you like this, Andrew?" Now they're both yelling at him.

Andrew grabs his girlfriend's hand and pulls her off the couch. "This is bullshit. I'm not fucking doing this."

They start to walk to the front door. Pop-pop, Philip, and

I stay where we are. I've never heard Andrew say bad words before. We're not even allowed to say *fart*.

"You know what?" my mother yells, "Fuck you!"

Smack!

Woah, Grandma slaps Jennie in the face for saying the F-word. Then she turns around and yells at Andrew. "Don't you dare talk like that in this house!"

This is the most bizarre fight I've ever seen. I think I'm in shock. It's all happening so fast. Our mother's here with her forced hugs, and now everyone's yelling. Andrew's leaving. Mom and Grandma yell at him until he's in his truck, driving away.

When they come back into the house, Jennie asks Philip to take her for a ride. "I've gotta get out of here," she says. "Can you just drive around somewhere?"

She leaves with Philip. They're gone for an hour, and later he tells me that she just cried the whole time. I spend that time hiding in Pop-pop's shed, sitting on the floor with my head on my knees and my arms wrapped around my legs, sobbing as hard as I've ever cried in my whole life. Grandma's in the house yelling at Pop-pop the whole time, and he lets her, I think so she doesn't come yell at me.

My mother isn't really coming back. She doesn't want us. We'll never be a real family.

Eventually, I hear Pop-pop and Philip calling my name. Pop-pop knows where I am, but they're giving me a chance to come out when I'm ready. I wipe my face and walk out front. I get in Philip's car, and we drive home with the windows down and his rap music rattling the car. I usually hate that feeling with the subwoofer thumping, but I don't mind today. It drowns everything out so I don't even have to hear myself think.

When we get home, Daddy's there. He asks, "How did it go?"

I know he can tell that I've been crying. I go to my room and cry some more. When I don't have any tears left, I start reading a book, even though my eyes hurt.

Andrew doesn't come home that night.

* * *

A few days have passed, and Daddy tells me, "Your grandparents called. Your mother went back to her new house."

I don't say anything. She left again. We only saw her once, and it was all yelling and tears. And now she's gone again.

"She lives in Maryland now," Daddy says.

Good, I think. *I'm glad she's gone. She was only back for like thirty minutes, and look at the trouble she caused.*

I'm used to her not being here. We don't feel like a family, but it was better with her gone. She just popped in, stirred everybody up, and left. No explanation and no apology. We're better off without her here.

The house feels heavy again. Daddy doesn't know exactly what happened, but he knows it wasn't good. Andrew is hardly home anymore, and Philip is angry all the time. We never talk about it. We just try to keep going.

* * *

I wait a few weeks for things to cool down, then I'm back at Grandma and Pop-pop's again. My brothers don't come, and not just because it isn't cool. They're still angry.

I'm hoping we don't have to talk about my mother, but Grandma starts right in.

"You were wrong to behave that way when your mother was here," she says.

"I didn't do anything," I tell her.

"Your mother just wanted to come visit all of you, and your brother was so nasty. It's wrong for him to be talking like that."

Pop-pop tells her to stop. She gets mad at him, and mad at me, but he protects me from her harsh words. Later, he has kind words for me. He tells me I'm the sweetest girl in the whole world.

Pop-pop must be so patient, just like my daddy. I kind of get it because I want my mother to like me and my grandmother to like me, too, but I want them to be nicer. I don't know if I can be as patient as Pop-pop and my daddy. I don't think I'll ever have a mom like my friends with normal families have, but maybe we can be friends on the phone. Maybe we can email.

I don't want her here. We're safer without her.

* * *

The rest of the summer goes by pretty fast. Daddy has another new chore that he's never done: school shopping. He takes me to the mall, gives me a hundred bucks, and says, "I'll wait right here. You just tell me when you're done." I think he does the same with Andrew and Philip.

Andrew's never home anymore. Philip spends most of his time at his friends' or in his room, and Daddy's always at work. I'm still volunteering at the church during the week. They have vacation Bible school and an afterschool program for kids whose parents work late. When the church moves because it's too big for the old church, they have a big youth group. They do fun things on weekends and sleepaway camps, and I always go to those.

Alyssa, a teacher who always seems to be looking out for me, has kind of taken me under her wing. I think she's about eighteen or nineteen, but she seems like an adult to me. She knows my mother's gone, so I think she's trying to sort of step in and help me out. She does special things, like pick me up at my house and take me to Orlando some weekends.

* * *

Even though I don't have a mom, I have people who love me and other people who sure seem to care a whole lot. I still have Daddy, and Andrew, and Philip, and Pop-pop, even if I don't get to spend a lot of time with them. It's not so bad. It could be worse.

Daddy's in charge of dinner every night, and we eat a lot of sub sandwiches from the sub shop and fried chicken from the grocery store, which I like. He makes chili for us—a couple cans of beans and tomatoes in the old Crock-Pot. Also rice and beans. I think that's all Daddy knows how to cook. I make my own snacks though, like sometimes after school I'll make a sandwich or macaroni and cheese. Things might not be up to our mother's standards, but they're good enough for us.

A few months have passed. I come home and no one else is there, just Daddy. He sits at his normal seat at the table, but he asks me to sit next to him, which isn't where I usually sit. I feel his knee touch mine, and I see that he's crying. I've never seen Daddy cry before. I'm scared. Something's wrong.

"As you know, your mother's not coming back. I've had to make the difficult decision to divorce her."

The church says you're not supposed to get divorced, except for infidelity. I know Daddy believes this. He and Jennie are married, for better or for worse. *Why is he doing this?*

That's when it hits me. *Oh, she must have cheated on him.*

Daddy is crying more. "I'm so sorry, Miss," he says. "I tried everything to prevent having to divorce your mother, but this is what has to happen. Part of our divorce says that I get to keep the house and you guys, so we don't have to move, and you don't have to change schools. You don't have to worry about that."

I wasn't even thinking about moving or changing schools. All I can think is, *Why doesn't she want us?*

I feel so abandoned. She told me she was only going to be gone for two weeks! And she hasn't called, not once. No letters, no chatroom talks on the internet. Nothing. But I still thought maybe she would come back. Instead, she betrayed us. All of us!

I'm crying too. Daddy says again, "I'm so sorry, Miss."

My heart hurts because I'm so sad and Daddy is so sad. I love him so much and I don't want him to hurt. That makes me cry harder.

This is all my fault. Maybe I could have done something so she didn't leave. I could have been nicer, quieter. She left because she hates me, and now Daddy is crying and I don't know what to do.

I stand up and run to my room. Slam the door and scream, "I want my mommy!" I'm wailing and wailing, crying my eyes out. I don't know what else to do. This hurts.

When my brothers get home, I don't say anything. They don't say anything either, but I feel like from now on, it's going to be a lot different. Not just because our mother's gone forever either. It's going to be different between my brothers and me too. Everybody is quiet. Andrew and Philip think their thoughts, and I think mine. We don't talk about them. We're all in the same house, and we sit down in the same kitchen for dinner, but it's like we're all living in different worlds that occasionally bump into each other. We just float through the house like ghosts.

Sometimes I hear my brothers yelling at each other in their bedroom. I go into my room and play loud, angry music to drown out their fighting. Daddy doesn't like Kid Rock, so that's what I play the most and the loudest. Sometimes he bangs on my door and says, "Turn it down!" Sometimes he doesn't even care.

CHAPTER 4

Life without Jennie

I CAN'T BELIEVE JENNIE'S BEEN GONE MORE THAN A year. I don't call her "Mommy" or "Mom" or even "my mother" anymore, even in my head. She's just Jennie, and I try not to think about her at all.

Today's a school day. I wake up early just like always, but I feel kind of funny in my stomach. *Am I sick? Food poisoning? The flu bug?* In the bathroom, there's blood. On me, in my underwear. I guess this is my period. *What am I going to do?*

My brothers are still asleep, but Daddy's at the kitchen table, eating breakfast and reading his Bible. I shuffle in, staring down at my feet. This is so embarrassing. I can't even look at Daddy. I know this is supposed to be normal, but no one told me what to do about periods, and I'm not prepared. *What do I say?*

I sit down on the other side of the table, my head down. I trace the lines in the wood with my finger and mumble, "I don't feel good, Daddy, and I don't want to go to school today."

Daddy stops eating. I keep my face down so he can't see

my eyes, but I'm pretty sure he's looking at me. His voice is different, serious, but kind.

"Do you need me to take the day off work and take you to the store?"

I can barely answer, but I get the word out. *Yes.*

"Okay. You go shower and get dressed. When K-Mart opens, I'll take you over there."

I'm so relieved that he didn't ask me any questions. I could never talk about it or say, *I got my period. I'm a girl and I got my period and I need help.* I don't want to talk about this with my dad—or with anyone. I'll shower and we'll just go and take care of this.

Daddy drives me to the store. He parks out front and hands me a five-dollar bill.

"I'll be right here when you're done, Miss," he says.

I have to go in the store all by myself. That's good, I think, because this is embarrassing. But I don't know what to look for. *Why didn't Jennie tell me about my period?*

I walk down all the aisles until I find the one I need. It's called "feminine hygiene." There's an entire wall of products, row after row after row of pink, purple, white, and blue. I look at all the shelves. Then I look at the five-dollar bill in my hand. *What do I need? And what can I get for five dollars?*

This is so embarrassing. I can feel my cheeks turning pink. If anyone walks down this aisle and sees me, I'll run away.

I find a big blue-and-white box that's less than five dollars. It's the store brand, and it says, "super-absorbent, nighttime sanitary napkins." That will last me the longest, I think. I don't know how long though, because I don't even know how much I'm going to bleed or how long my period is going to last.

I walk to the checkout line with the box tucked to my side so no one can see it. After the person in front of me leaves, I put the box on the counter. I don't look at the lady at the register. She scans the box, and I throw the money down and run out. I don't even wait for the change or my receipt. I hop in the car. "Let's go, Daddy," I say quietly. He doesn't say a word.

* * *

Daddy takes me to lunch at Bono's. I order chicken fingers and french fries, my favorite. My father gets a barbecue pork sandwich on a bun. We don't talk about what's happening with my body; we just hang out and eat. It feels good to be sitting here with him, and the embarrassment is starting to fade. I'm so happy and proud to have such a good daddy.

Daddy did okay today, and I did okay too. I'm a little worried that there might be other things that I don't know about, but there's nothing I can do about that now. I guess I'll just wait and see. It would be nice to have someone I could ask, like a mother, but I'm not going to think about that now.

* * *

I'm still involved with the church some, volunteering, and doing some activities with the other girls my age. The youth pastor and his wife, Melissa, have three kids, two boys and a girl. I babysit for them all the time. Melissa and all the other women at the church are nice to me. They know I don't have a mother, and I get the feeling they want to help, but they don't know what to say or do. It's awkward sometimes, being the only kid without a mom.

The church is having a mother-daughter luncheon. They're doing a fashion show, and some of the moms and daughters are going to walk the runway together, like models. I want to go, but I can't. It's just one more thing I'm missing out on. Jennie has been gone a year and a half.

Melissa asks me to stay after youth group. She's holding her littlest one, a cute baby boy, and bouncing him on her lap. He's giggling away.

"The luncheon is going to be a lot of fun, Emily. Since I don't have a daughter who's old enough to go, how about you and I go together?"

She's making it seem like I'm doing her a favor, and that helps me feel a little less pathetic. It's nice to be invited, but it's sad, too, because we both know the real reason she's asking me. We both know my situation.

"Um, yes, sure," I say.

I meet Melissa at the church. We eat lunch together and all the other girls are there with their moms, doing crafts, laughing, and having a good time. Melissa and I sit together for the fashion show, but we don't walk the runway. That would be too much. This is nice. This is enough.

Everyone's paying attention to the show, and I go into the church bathroom. I sit in a stall and cry very quietly. I don't want anyone to know that I'm crying, but I miss my mom. No, I just miss *having* a mom. I wish I had a real mom who wanted to be here with me.

I wipe my face with some toilet paper and flush it down the toilet so it sounds like I used the bathroom for real. Then I wash my hands and put on some ChapStick. I push the corners of my mouth up into a happy face, like I'm having a good time. Just like all the other girls, the ones with moms.

At home, I cry some more. It feels like I didn't get it all out earlier. I may never get it all out.

* * *

It's been six months since I've seen Jennie. Six months since the blowup. Six months since I found out she's never coming back. I don't want her to come back. Not like that. She'll never be the mother I hoped for, or even the mother she was before. It's all a mess now, and it's better if she stays away. But I don't know what comes next.

Daddy works a lot and keeps the house together, tries to keep the family together. Philip hangs out with his friends, and since Andrew got his license he's always gone. My brothers are angry all the time. No one sees me. We don't see each other. I feel like a ghost in the house, just...existing. We don't eat meals together or even talk anymore. I feel like the only time we communicate is when we're fighting, and I don't even know what we fight about. Stupid stuff. They're so angry and I'm scared.

I stop going to church, and I don't do any of the volunteer work I used to do. I still go to school most days, but then I come home and watch TV, maybe read a book, and go to bed. This is my life, and it's lonely. It's hard. I spend so much time alone with my feelings—my horrible, awful feelings. I don't like being alone, but I can't let anyone in. I'm afraid of what they'll think of me, how they'll judge me. What they'll do to me. And I'm afraid of what might happen if I'm alone too long.

I don't know if I'll make it through high school, or even to eighteen, seventeen, sixteen. I cry about this a lot. I cry about everything. I don't even know why I'm crying—it just hurts, and I want to let the pain out.

Tonight was rough. Andrew came home for a while and yelled at me, and I yelled back. Then he left again. I'm hurting, and I want to hurt something back. I get a steak knife from the kitchen, go into my bedroom closet, and pull the door shut. I'm four years old again, sitting in the dark, knees pulled up to my chin. I lean against the toy box that my Pop-pop made for me, bury my face in my knees, and sob. I cry until there are no tears left, and now I'm just alone with my pain. I have to let it out.

I wipe my face on my arm and notice the steak knife is still in my hand. I touch the serrated blade to my forearm and draw it over the skin. A thin white line appears. I do it again, this time pressing down on the blade so hard that it pierces the skin. A red line appears, and a thin stream of blood trickles down my arm. I feel...Surprise. I feel...*Relief.*

This is my pain.

Somehow, seeing the blood, this pain on my flesh—*outside of my body*—validates it. Makes it real. My pain is real. It *is* real.

My sadness is real, my loneliness, my worthlessness, and my shame. I make more cuts—four, five, six. Short little cuts and not too deep. Just enough to ease the pain. Thoughts run through my head, the same thoughts that haunt me day in and day out, and now I'm saying them out loud.

It's all my fault. It's all my fault. It's all my fault.

Cut. Cut. Cut.

I'm worthless. I'm alone. I'm afraid.

Then I cut my other arm.

* * *

I can't believe I did this. Everyone will see the cuts and think there's something wrong with me. I put on a sweater to cover them up. Some of the kids at school ask me how I can be wearing a long-sleeve sweater when it's so hot out, and I say, "Oh, I know, but I'm just a little cold." I don't like lying, but I can't show them my arms.

It felt so good when I was doing it, but now I feel like garbage. I'm a terrible person who can't even get through normal teenage life, can't control my emotions. *Why did I do this to myself?* I feel guilty, like I did something really wrong. No one can know. I tell no one. Ever.

Even though I feel bad, I do it again. Not every day, but at least once a week. Just on the really bad days. When someone at school makes fun of me. When I get into an argument with my daddy. When I'm overwhelmed with worthlessness.

It's all my fault!

I'm not good enough. Not good enough to deserve a mother or a real family. Not good enough for anything.

I wish someone would show me the way out of this life, but I can't let anyone in. I build a brick wall inside me, and no one is getting past it. I'm not going to be vulnerable and let anyone in just for them to hurt me. I don't even know what to do with the hurt that I have.

I keep cutting myself for a year.

* * *

I'm hanging out more with Kim now—going to the park, walking the running trails in our neighborhood, and working out on the outdoor exercise equipment.

I'm learning more about her too. Kim's mother is an addict and an alcoholic, but her parents got divorced a long time ago, and Kim's dad got custody of her. She had a baby brother when her parents were married, but he died when he was very young. Kim's dad remarried, and now she has a stepmom, a stepbrother, and a little sister—her dad and stepmom's little girl.

Kim's stepmom is awful. She's mean to her, and she says things to make Kim feel bad. Sometimes she hurts her—physically hurts her. I think this is why Kim doesn't like to go home. I don't like to go home either, so we're hanging out a lot lately.

Most days we stay out until dinnertime. I feel like we're helping each other.

I'm not alone anymore, and I stop cutting myself. The marks heal and I can stop hiding them. I can stop hiding me, too, because I tell Kim everything.

Every day, we're together. We both get bicycles and ride all over town. Sometimes we go to IHOP. Having someone like Kim to talk to is the best, even better than Pop-pop, because she's my age. *Is this what it's like to have a friend?*

Kim introduces me to her friend Sarah. Sarah has a really cool house near the high school, where we all go to school. There's always candy in the pantry at Sarah's, and she has dogs. There's even a pond in her backyard. It's the perfect after-school hangout.

I'm over there today with Kim, and Sarah's mother comes home from work. It's the first time we've met, and I notice she's very tiny, very petite, with long, really dark hair. She's so pretty!

Sarah introduces us. "Hey, Mom, this is Emily. Emily, this is my mom, Jill."

"Hi, Jill," I say, "It's nice to meet you."

Oh my gosh, I'm thinking, *I called Sarah's mother, an adult, by her first name! Ugh.* I feel stupid.

Jill must see the look on my face because she smiles at me and says, "Call me Mom!"

Okay, I think, *that's even weirder.*

"Everyone who comes to the house calls me Mom," she explains, "That's just who I am!"

I can't call her Mom. It just doesn't feel right. I don't say anything else about it, but whenever I'm at Sarah's house and Jill's there, I just say, "hello," or "goodbye," without saying Jill, or Mrs. Stiriz, or Mom.

* * *

Sarah's house is still our after-school hangout, and now Kim and I spend every weekend there, too, from Friday afternoon until Sunday. We even spend some nights there during the week. Sarah's dad, Russell, lives and works in North Carolina, so it's just us girls. We talk about boys, clothes, having our periods, and shaving our legs—all those things I can't talk about at my house.

Jill likes the company for Sarah, and I think for herself too. She loves being a mom and treating us well. We get to stay up as late as we want and watch whatever we want on TV. Jill makes all the foods we like, too, like macaroni and cheese. She lets us have Coca-Cola, which is a real treat. We never have soda at our house.

She's playful, too, and makes me laugh. "Okay, girls," she'll say, "I'm going to the grocery store. What do you think? Should I get more chocolate chip cookies?"

We all chime in the same, "Of course! More chocolate chip cookies, please!"

My daddy asks me why I'm hardly ever home anymore, and I tell him about Sarah's house and about Jill. "Kim and I like it there," I say, "Sarah has a really cool mom." I think he gets it because he doesn't ask me again.

Jill asks about my family life sometimes, but she never presses me for details, especially if she can tell I'm uncomfortable. "Never mind. Let's change the subject," she says.

She likes to tease us about hanging around so much. "Girls, wouldn't you rather go to a party or something tonight?" she says. "I can drop you off and then pick you up later."

We all look at her and laugh. "Nope," we tell her, "We like it here."

It's true. We all feel safe at Sarah's house, especially with Jill there.

* * *

I'm dating now, in ninth grade. I have a few different boyfriends in high school, but nothing serious. They all have nice families. I spend a lot of time at their homes hanging out with their moms and sisters. It's almost like being part of a real family. It's not perfect though.

School isn't as interesting to me anymore, and I skip a lot of days in my sophomore year. I don't know how I manage to pass into eleventh grade. After a while, I stop going completely. My life is pretty good, between dating, hanging out at my boyfriend's house, and spending the rest of my time at Sarah's. I even call Jill "Mom" now. It's like Kim and Sarah and Jill and I are a family. A family of girls.

* * *

Kim is always telling her dad that she's going to move out when she turns eighteen. I get the feeling he doesn't believe her though. She asks me to come over on her eighteenth birthday because she's really going to do it. I go to her house, where she has all her belongings stuffed into big plastic bags, the kind you use to clean up the lawn.

Kim tells me that her dad came in her room that morning to give her a birthday present and saw all the bags. She told him she was moving out that day and couldn't pick up her little sister after school. He must have thought she was bluffing because he and Kim's stepmom went to work. But here we are now, loading all of Kim's stuff into her Explorer and my truck. A couple of our guy friends, Steven and Chris, are here to help too. We get all the bags into the vehicles and drive to Jill's house. Kim moves into her guest room.

* * *

One night, Kim and I go to a house party in another town. I meet this guy there, Jeff, and we start dating. Pretty soon he's my new boyfriend, and the next thing I know, I'm moving out of my house and in with him. Fort Pierce is a long drive from Jill's house, and from Kim and Sarah, but I guess it's time I grow up and make my own family. I get a full-time job managing a tanning salon. Jeff works for his uncle, hanging wallpaper.

The salon has a lot of mirrors on the walls so people can see their tans. I'm more aware of how I look, and I don't like it. I'm average. Totally average.

One weekend I'm visiting Sarah, and I tell her how I feel.

"Ugh, I'm so fat," I say.

"You are not!" she says, "You look great, Emily. You don't need to lose weight."

I decide to eat less food, and pretty soon I lose a few pounds. It feels good to see my body respond so quickly—like I did something and got an immediate result. Like I'm *in control.*

I want more of that feeling, so I eat less and less. Sometimes I don't eat for days. When we order lunch from the Chinese restaurant next door to the tanning salon, I only get white rice. I count the grains I eat, trying to eat one less grain each time. I eat just enough to stop the growling in my stomach and quell the hunger pangs. Then I can go another day without eating.

That's what I did this week. I ate a little bit of rice, just a handful of grains, yesterday—nothing today. I get home and I'm so hungry that I open a new bag of potato chips and stuff them in my mouth, one at a time. One after another, after another, until the whole bag's gone. After that I feel sick to my stomach.

Jeff comes home from work and finds the empty bag. "Whoa," he says, "You ate the whole bag of chips!"

"I was hungry," I tell him. "I didn't have a chance to eat all day because we were so busy." That's a lie, but Jeff believes me. I decide to keep lying to him about my eating. If he makes dinner before I come home, I tell him, "Oh, I ate right before I left work."

I don't even know why I'm doing this anymore. I'm not fat. I think I want someone to notice. I want someone to stop me. I can't stop myself. I get down to ninety-eight pounds, and still, no one notices. I wear baggy T-shirts to cover up the weight loss.

One day, I'm getting out of the shower when Jeff walks in. I can tell by the look on his face that he's kind of shocked. He can see my backbone, my ribs.

"Emily," he says," "What's going on? You're so skinny. Too skinny."

I mumble something about not having much of an appetite lately and figure that's the end of it.

* * *

Every couple of weeks, we go to Jeff's grandmother's house for dinner. It's kind of a tradition. Tonight his whole family is there, just like always.

I do my usual trick, pretending to eat, but mostly pushing the food around on my plate. I take an occasional bite, chew slowly, then secretly spit the food out in my napkin. No one notices, just like always. After faking it for a while, maybe twenty minutes or so, I clear my plate. We all sit back down for dessert, and of course I say, "No thank you, I'm full."

Everyone's looking at me. *Why are they looking at me?* Jeff's uncle clears his throat.

"Emily," he says, "It's come to our attention that you've lost a lot of weight and you might be dealing with something. We're concerned, and we want to help you."

They know. They noticed. They *care*. Jeff's uncle continues. "We really do want to help you, but we want to give you the opportunity to help yourself first. We love you, Emily. Please start eating again. We don't want anything bad to happen to you; we just want you to get better."

"Okay," I say, surprised and a little embarrassed. I can feel my face getting warm. This isn't a bad feeling though. They *care*. "I guess I'll take a little of that dessert."

Eating food every day takes some time. My stomach has shrunk so much, but little by little, I'm eating more and more. I'm feeling so much better, and not just because of the food.

I feel seen. I feel cared for. I feel *loved*.

* * *

Jeff and I get engaged and start planning our wedding. We've been living together for five years now, and it seems like the logical next step. We love each other so much, and we're so happy. Why not?

Daddy and Mary have been dating for a long time, too, and they finally get married. Mary's moving to Florida to be with him. They seem really happy together, and I'm happy for them. I hope it's the same for Jeff and me.

It's not though. Being married is harder than I thought it would be. *Maybe I was too young to do this. Maybe we both weren't ready.* We separate and try living apart for over a year, then we try being together again. No matter how much we love each other, it just doesn't work.

After another big fight, I tell Jeff I'm leaving and I want a divorce. He helps me pack my stuff, and I leave my husband— just like my biological mother did. At least we don't have kids, but I can't help thinking: *Please, please, please, Emily, I cannot turn into Jennie.*

I feel like a complete failure. The guilt consumes me, and it's worse because I haven't only pushed Jeff away—his whole family stops speaking to me. I understand their anger, and some days I regret my decision. *Why couldn't I have done better? Tried harder? Not given up so quickly?*

Everything I do fails. I failed as a daughter and that's why my mother left. Failed at high school and never graduated. Failed at marriage and now I'm alone. Is there anything I can do right? It doesn't feel like it. Some days I don't even know why I'm still here. I'm just one big mistake. And just like always, with every new failure, it's all my fault.

CHAPTER 5

Brent

AFTER THE DIVORCE, I DATE A FEW BOYS, BUT NOTHING serious. Then I meet this guy Seth. He's so charming and very confident—everything I'm not. We're hanging around more and more often, and before I know it, we're in a relationship. I feel like I have a real boyfriend for once. Today Seth and I are going to the beach. We're meeting my friend Matt there. I know Matt from my job at the restaurant, and he's been one of my best friends for a long time.

Matt has a guy with him I've never seen before, Brent. He's in the military and visiting Matt while he's on temporary leave from his assignment. The two of them grew up together. Brent's very good-looking and funny too. We sort of click immediately, which is uncomfortable with Seth standing right there. I kind of wish I had met him sooner. But I'm in a serious relationship with Seth, and besides, Brent's in the military and will be leaving soon. I can't think about Brent right now, but sometimes I do anyway.

* * *

Seth got a job in California, and I guess I'm going with him. I'm excited but worried too. Something isn't right. Seth isn't as nice to me as he was at first. He doesn't like me hanging out with my friends or spending time with my family. He doesn't even like me working. I've been modeling bathing suits for Body Glove for a few years, and even though it's part time, the paycheck's great. I really like the people, and I can keep modeling for them when I move to California.

I tell myself that Seth just wants me all to himself because he likes me so much. I tell myself he just needs me, and I should be there for him. That's what people in a relationship do, right? *If I were a good girlfriend and really cared about him, I would be willing to make sacrifices. I would be willing to put his needs ahead of my own sometimes, like now, when he's starting a new job.* He's probably just stressed out and feeling a little insecure. I'll stand by him because I want to be a good girlfriend. This is probably just a temporary thing, and once we move and he settles into the new job, everything will go back to normal.

* * *

In California, things aren't getting better between Seth and me. They're worse. *He* is worse. He doesn't care how he makes me feel, and he makes me feel bad. He isn't just stressed out—he's mean. He's emotionally abusive. Everything always has to be about him and how wonderful and smart he is. Everything about me is wrong, and he tells me how wrong I am every day.

Seth's words remind me of Jennie. They remind me of that old voice in my head that used to tell me that everything was my fault. Seth's words and actions, no matter how painful, are what I'm used to. Maybe that's why I stay. If I just love him enough and wait long enough, he'll go back to the Seth I met in Florida—the charming, confident guy who was so nice. That guy who complimented me all the time and went out of his way to make me feel special.

I mean, he was good to me, right? For a while, anyway. But now that I think about it, he stopped being nice before we left Florida. There were good days and bad days, but Seth had reasons for the bad days. His job was stressful. He's probably still going through a stressful time, and things will go back to normal soon.

* * *

I get a job at a restaurant working the breakfast shift. Maybe I'll make some friends. I meet a few people and they invite me to hang out after work, but when I tell Seth, he wants to know why. Why am I hanging out? Why can't I just go home and do the housework and make his dinner? I get out of work at 3 o'clock so there's plenty of time to make dinner, but I can tell he doesn't want me going out. After a few months, I quit the job.

I still have my Body Glove gig. I am not giving that up.

* * *

Seth and I belong to a gym. He's really into bodybuilding, so I go with him and we work out together every day. I follow Seth from one machine to the next and he tells me which exercises to do. There are so many men at the gym, and I'm afraid I might accidentally look at one of them, and that would upset Seth. I keep my head down. On leg day, when Seth does squats, I sit on a bench and watch him so he knows I'm not looking at anyone else.

After the gym, we go home and Seth takes a shower. I

prepped his dinner before we went to the gym, and now, while Seth showers, I finish cooking it or warm it up. This way, he doesn't have to wait to eat. Seth doesn't like to wait for his dinner.

* * *

Seth is getting worse. I think he hates me. He says he loves me, but I don't feel loved at all. I feel like the worst person in the world when I'm around him. Seth likes to throw every failure, every mistake I've ever made, in my face: "Look at you, in your twenties and already divorced," he says. He says I can't cook or do laundry either. Everything I do is wrong.

When he's not around, I think about what he's putting me through, and I want it to stop, but I don't know what to do, and I don't know who or how to ask for help.

I stop calling and texting my friends and family because it makes him mad. At first, I think he's jealous and wants me all to himself. It feels good to have someone want me. But now, I don't know. It doesn't feel like he wants me. More like he doesn't want anyone else to have me, and he just wants, what? To make me feel bad? That doesn't make sense. People don't do that, do they? I mean, most people. Not the people I love, and I love Seth.

The fighting has gotten worse. Almost every day we're screaming at each other. Seth throws things at me and there are marks on the walls. I want to fix this, so I ask Seth if we can see a counselor.

"This isn't working, Seth," I say, "Let's get a therapist and work on it together. We still love each other so much, and it would be worth it. We can get back to where we were before."

Maybe the therapist can show me what I'm doing wrong.

Maybe they can teach me to be the kind of girlfriend who'll make Seth happy again. Make him love me again.

* * *

Seth won't go to the therapist's office, but he agrees to see him online. Today is our third session. The laptop is set up on the dining room table, and the therapist is talking to Seth about how his behavior contributes to our fights. Seth will not take responsibility—he does not like being held accountable. He explains to the therapist why he acts the way he does.

"Sometimes Emily doesn't make my lunch the way I like it," he says. "And you should see how she puts away my laundry. It's no wonder we have problems."

When it's just the two of us at home, Seth has all the control. Here, even though the therapist isn't physically in the room, he has control of the conversation. He doesn't accept Seth's excuses, and he doesn't blame me for Seth's behavior. I keep expecting Seth to blow up at him, but he doesn't; he keeps his cool. But I can see his face, and I know he isn't happy.

I don't think this is working.

The session ends and Seth blows up at me. He says this whole therapy thing is just a setup to make him take the blame for everything. He says I'm crazy and that our problems are not his fault. *How many times has Seth told me I'm crazy? How long has he been telling me that? When did I start to believe him?*

Seth doesn't want to see the therapist anymore, and I don't want to deal with the fights after therapy, so we quit. He still talks about it though—about how I made him go to therapy with me because I'm crazy. *Am I?*

I don't know what to do. I've been in California for almost five months now. I'm thousands of miles away from everyone

I know, everyone who cares about me. I have to figure this out, but it's so hard.

I can't think about this right now. Let's just see how things go.

* * *

Several months have passed since those therapy sessions. Seth and I made it through the holidays, but nothing has changed. I start connecting with Kim again, back in Florida. I can't do this by myself anymore. I am so alone.

Kim and I FaceTime a lot—sometimes, on her days off, we talk all day. We call it "wine time FaceTime" because we drink wine on our calls. I drink a little some days, and some days I drink a lot. I'm telling Kim about my life with Seth. She doesn't judge me. She just says, "Why don't you just come home? You can stay with me."

She doesn't push me though. Kim knows that leaving has to be my decision, but she's afraid for me, and she wants to help. I think about what she says.

But springtime is coming, and I'm hopeful that everything will be better between Seth and me this year. I don't have my own money. All I have is Seth, and leaving would be so hard.

* * *

Another bad fight. It started in the kitchen and now we're in the living room. *What are we fighting about?* I don't remember. We're always arguing, and it's always about something trivial— some insignificant thing that I did or I said that set Seth off. He hurls a coffee cup at me and misses. It smashes against the wall and there's glass everywhere. Great, another dent in the wall too.

Our apartment's tiny but I have to get away. I go into the bedroom and start packing a bag. I don't know where I'm going but I have to leave. It's dark out and I have no money and nowhere to go. I'll just go outside and sit in the car.

I'm sitting on the bed, stuffing clothes into a suitcase, when Seth comes in. He grabs my arms. He's never put his hands on me, not like this. I don't even see it coming—don't see him raise his hand, don't see it coming at my face.

Smack. He hits me, and something inside me breaks. Not a physical thing but something that's been keeping me here. Whatever was holding me to this place, to Seth, just broke. I kick at him, screaming, and he lets go of my arms.

Seth has this weird look on his face. He doesn't look angry anymore. He leaves the room.

I'm sobbing as I finish packing my suitcase. I grab my keys and get my dog Liko because I'm afraid that if I'm not there, Seth could hurt the dog. He never has, but he's never hit me before either.

I sit up front in the car and try to sleep. At 4:30 in the morning, I go inside. I lie on the couch and wait for the sun to come up.

This is not right. This is not love. This is not what I want for my life.

It's over. I'm leaving.

* * *

It's three hours later on the East Coast, so I call my brother Andrew in New York. I tell him I'm leaving California and I need five hundred dollars for gas, food, and motels. He transfers the money to my bank account, no questions asked. My brothers and I have loaned the same five hundred dollars to each other for years, and I had loaned Andrew the money a couple of years ago. We all bank with Wells Fargo and know each other's account numbers, so we can transfer the money back and forth.

Seth is getting ready for work. My suitcase is full, and I start packing everything else in garbage bags. My dog Liko, an Irish setter mix, takes up the whole back seat of my tiny Honda Civic, so I can only take what fits in the passenger seat and the trunk. I have a few bags, a plastic bin full of pictures, and a folder with my important documents, like my birth certificate.

Seth asks what I'm doing, and I tell him I'm leaving. For once, I'm not crying though. I don't ever want him to see me cry again.

Seth shrugs his shoulders like "whatever." He doesn't believe me—thinks I'm just being dramatic. I'm not though. He leaves for work.

I grab my toothbrush, Liko, and the dog food, and I'm gone.

* * *

It's a long drive from Santa Cruz to Kim's house in Florida. Kim says that my room, "Emily's room," she calls it, will be ready for me when I get there and that she even washed the sheets.

My route takes me through Texas, and I remember that a friend of mine from the restaurant, Becky, moved to Houston a while ago. I find her number in my phone and call to see if I can stay at her place for a night. When I get to Becky's, I'm exhausted. I've only been driving for two days, but I'm physically and emotionally drained. We sit on the couch, watch movies, and eat popcorn. I'd forgotten how wonderful this was, to sit with a friend.

For the first time in a very long time, I can breathe. I take the deepest breaths and let them out slowly. I'm ashamed and embarrassed, but I'm not afraid anymore. I did the right thing. Finally, I did the right thing for me.

At night, I sleep. I sleep so hard.

I stay at Becky's for three days.

* * *

I'm back in Florida—*home*. I feel safe here, not like I felt with Seth. Safe, but a mess, too, because there must be something really wrong with me to stay with a guy like that for so long. I should have left the first time he called me a name, the first time he hurt me. Before he had a chance to hit me. Who stays in a relationship with a person like that? *My daddy did*, I think, *for a long time.* This is what I know. Jennie didn't hit Daddy, but she hurt him with her words and her actions. She hurt him with her treatment of my brothers and me. I can't think about that right now. I have to figure out who I am and what I'm going to do with my life.

Seth texts me every day. He doesn't apologize or ask me to come back. His words are mean. And I...I text him back. I say that maybe we can work things out. We could try a long-distance relationship.

But he doesn't want me anymore.

What am I doing? What am I thinking? I block Seth's number on my phone. Then I block him and his whole family on all my social media. I need to make a clean break from the emotional side of our relationship so I can see it with a clear head.

Who have I become, and what am I going to do with my life now?

One thing's for sure: I'm staying single. All my relationships have failed, and it's no wonder, because I'm basically incapable of having a healthy one. Being single will have to be the way I live my life from now on. It's better to be alone than to go through another Seth. So what if I don't follow the usual social norms? So what if I don't get married and have kids?

I'll just be alone.

* * *

I have found something I'm very good at, and that's work. Before I left for California, I was working as a busser at a fine dining restaurant, the one where I met Matt. Over time, I had worked my way up to server. Now that I'm in Florida again, they hire me back right away. The money's great, and the people are fantastic. The best part is how good I feel when I'm there. Seth destroyed my self-esteem. Every day was unpredictable, and I never knew what he would do next to hurt me. This is so different. It's like being part of a big family when I'm at work, and I'm there as much as possible. The people like me, and there are no surprises.

I still have my part-time gig as a swimsuit model for Body Glove. I walk the runway so retailers can decide what they're going to order for their shops. I travel around, doing six to ten live shows a year. My boss at the restaurant is flexible with my hours and lets me have time off for the shows, knowing I'll be right back there as soon as I can, working full time like always. Sometimes, when I'm up on the runway with all those people looking at me, I can't help remembering that not so many years ago, I was skinny as a rail. Those ninety-eight-pound days are behind me, but I still feel a little out of place with all those pretty girls on stage. *How did I get up here?*

Working all the time keeps me from being alone. I hate being by myself. On the rare times when I am alone, thoughts creep into my head. I think about all my past failures. I think about my family. I think about Jennie.

My high school friend, Kim, has a house now, and she and her boyfriend let me rent a room in it. I'm paying my own way, and I even pay off my car. I'm on my own, debt free, and saving money for the future. Just like an adult. I am an adult—twenty-seven years old. Maybe I'm not such a failure after all.

* * *

Not dating is easy. There's no pressure at all. I work, I make money, I pay my bills. I have a great work life, and I still have plenty of friends to hang out with when I don't want to be alone. I'm hanging out with my friend Matt tonight, and guess who he brought along. That guy Brent, from the beach. The guy who's in the military. The one that I clicked with so quickly. We get to talking, and I learn that he's married but he and his wife have separated.

"It's hard on military families, when you're gone all the time," he tells me. Brent's been deployed to Afghanistan twice. It sounds like there's no animosity between him and his wife— they just drifted apart.

The attraction between the two of us is palpable. *Of course, I want to date him, but how does he feel about it?*

We start hanging out on our own, without Matt, and pretty soon we're dating. Brent's still in the military, and he's in college too. He's also working through a divorce, and I don't want to get in the middle of that. I'm not even looking for a serious relationship, especially after the one I just got out of with Seth. I don't trust men. I don't even trust myself anymore. I thought I was a pretty good judge of character, but I'm not. How else did I end up with a guy like that? And why did I stay so long? I can't do that again, so I'm keeping it casual with Brent. I think I like being single. I just don't want to be alone.

Today we're camping on the prairie with a group of friends. Brent's parents are here.

"This is Emily," he tells them, "She's my girlfriend."

What? Girlfriend? When did that happen, and why wasn't I notified?

"I'm not your girlfriend!" I snap back, playfully.

"Of course you're my girlfriend," he says, "And we're going to get married someday."

I don't know how I feel about this. On the one hand, it's exciting to have this wonderful man feel so sure about me. He's all in, and he doesn't even know me—not all of me. On the other hand, it's scary. *Once he gets to know all of me, will he still call me his girlfriend?*

I can't deal with another failure. I've come too far, and I'm not doing it again.

"No," I insist, "I'm *not* your girlfriend." Brent just smiles.

I'm worried about failing this relationship. I'm worried about Brent too. He seems too good to be true. I've dated guys in the past who seemed great at first—attentive, caring, like they were crazy about me. But after a while, once they thought they had me—like I was in love with them or something—everything changed. They turned out to be controlling, abusive nutcases. *Is Brent one of those nutcases? A sociopath, even?* Because this can't be real. A guy this nice can't like me this much. There has to be a catch.

I'll keep dating him, I tell myself, *and watch for the red flags.* And I won't be his girlfriend. That way, as soon as he starts to change—starts bossing me around and telling me what to do, what to wear, where to go—I'll break it off. And if it turns out he's actually normal, he's eventually going to realize that I'm a mess, and he'll be the one to break it off. Either way, as long as I keep my distance—at least emotionally—he can't hurt me. I have to protect myself. As much as I like Brent, *and I like him a lot*, I can't fully trust him.

* * *

So maybe I am Brent's girlfriend. I feel like his girlfriend, but I would never tell him that. I don't want to get locked into something. I like being single.

He treats me so well though. No red flags, not like some other guys I've dated who started out nice, then I found out they weren't so nice. Some were controlling, and some didn't seem to care about me. If I were going to be somebody's girlfriend, Brent would make a good boyfriend.

He knows that I like to fish and that I've been on a mission to catch a snook. He borrows a friend's boat and some fishing gear, and we're off to some river in Melbourne, about an hour up the coast. It turns out he doesn't have the right bait, we're not in the right canal, and it isn't the right time of day to be fishing, but all that doesn't matter. The fact that Brent made the effort to take me snook fishing makes me giddy.

"Look," I tell him, "this is a lot of fun and I'm happy to be out here with you on the water. But I'm going to have to teach you how to fish!"

We're both laughing, and now we're kissing, and I can't believe this man likes me. He likes *me*.

We see each other every day now, and he isn't changing. There is no other side to Brent. He's the sweetest, kindest, most generous man I've ever known. Sometimes while I'm at work, he takes my car to be detailed and brings it back before my shift ends. I'm not used to this, and I'm letting my guard down. Can

I trust this man? I can. I will. I'm in love, but I won't tell him—not yet. Not even when his divorce is final. I keep it to myself.

* * *

Brent's finally graduating from college. Next is quartermaster school in Virginia for sixteen weeks, then he's off to Fort Carson, Colorado. He has a few weeks off before he leaves for Virginia, and we haven't talked about what's going to happen with "us" or if there will even be an "us." *Will we keep dating? Will this be a long-distance thing? Or...what?* I don't know. I get the feeling he expects me to just come with him, but he hasn't asked me. We haven't even talked about it.

Instead, we're going on a cruise to the Bahamas. *Is this a final goodbye?* I don't know.

Brent asks me to go to Virginia with him, and I agree. It's a relief to know what's next. Or is it? We haven't discussed any of the details, like where I'm going to stay in Virginia. We don't even live together now. *What about my friends? What about work? What is the long-term plan anyway? Am I just going for a visit, or to stay?* Maybe we'll discuss it on this cruise. At this point, we're spending every night together, and I've finally worked up the courage to tell him I love him. So, maybe the cruise, and a few weeks in Virginia, and that's it? I don't know.

For now, I'm just going to enjoy our time together. After all, Brent's in celebration mode. His divorce is final, and he's done with college and ready for quartermaster school and his new career in Colorado. He has a lot of work ahead of him—long hours with the military—and he needs a break. I don't want to mess this up for him or make him feel pressured to commit to anything past Virginia. I don't want to commit to anything either.

* * *

I thought I'd love being on a boat, especially with all the fishing I did as a kid, but I'm seasick the whole time. I'm so nauseous, I feel like I'm going to die. Even the Dramamine barely helps. On top of everything else, I'm supposed to get my period too. *Great.* But I don't get it, and I tell myself it's the boat, and the stress, and the seasickness. After the cruise, I still don't get it. Now I'm worried.

Could I be pregnant? Of course I could. I'm not even on birth control, and we don't use protection. I've tried things in the past—pills, shots—but they make my hormones go crazy. One pill made me cry all the time, for no reason at all. *Does Brent know I'm not on birth control?* I must have told him.

I tell him what's going on—that I'm late, and I'm worried—and he's totally cool about it. I feel so stupid, so reckless. I should have been more careful. Now, I have to know. I get a pregnancy test at the drug store and later that day, while he's in the garage packing, I go in the bathroom and take the test.

I'm in shock. *How did this happen?* I know darn well how it happened. *Okay, so how do I tell Brent?*

I walk out to the garage and wait for Brent to look up, to look at me.

"I'm going to have to go to the doctor," I say. I can't even get the words out: *I'm pregnant.*

Brent goes back to packing. "Okay," he says. That's it. I'm terrified. *Okay? What does that mean?*

I go back in the house and put on my swimsuit. We're supposed to be meeting some friends at the beach. *How long will I be able to wear this suit?* I can't believe I'm even thinking about this. I can't believe I'm pregnant!

On the drive, Brent asks me why I'm so stressed.

Finally, I blurt it out. "Because I'm pregnant!"

"Well at least we know the equipment works," he says, jokingly.

I laugh nervously. Then I say, "This is serious, Brent." It is serious. It's my body. It's my life.

"You're going to be fine," he says, putting his hand on my thigh and giving it a squeeze. "There's no reason to stress, Emily. You'll be okay. *We're* going to be okay."

He holds my hand the rest of the way. At the beach, it's like nothing just happened. Like we didn't just find out I'm pregnant, and we're going to be parents, and our lives will never be the same. *How can he be so calm?*

I'm not calm. Not calm at all. I feel like a mouse in a trap. I love Brent and the thought of having a life with him. *But a baby? A tiny person that I have to take care of?*

I don't know how to be a mom. I'm just figuring out how to be an adult! And a girlfriend! A baby will change my whole life, and I don't know if I can do this.

* * *

I'm still not used to the idea of being pregnant, but I have to plan for it. Brent and I agree that after Virginia, I'll be moving to Colorado with him. I don't want to raise a baby alone. Then I give my notice at the restaurant. This isn't the first time I've moved away, and like always, they tell me that whenever I move back, my job will be waiting for me.

I want to talk to someone besides Brent about this, but who? I text one of my restaurant friends who has two kids of her own. When she responds with "I'm so happy for you" and "You must be so excited," I text back, "No, I'M FREAKING OUT!"

I *am* freaking out. I'm not ready for this—not ready to be

a mom. I don't know if I will ever be ready. I've said so many times that I don't want kids, and I've meant it. Not because I don't like kids, because I do. I'm just afraid that I could be a bad mom. I don't ever want to put a child through the pain that Jennie inflicted on my brothers and me, and how do I know that I won't?

But I am going to be a mom, and now I have to deal with that fact. I don't even know where to start. I'm nervous about telling anyone, especially my friends. This will change my whole life, including my relationship with Kim, Sarah, and Jill. No more going to the beach. No more lunches with the girls. No more cocktails.

I think about my parents. I haven't spoken to Jennie in years, and I don't even know if I want to tell her. I have to tell Daddy. *How am I going to do that? What is he going to think of me?*

* * *

Brent and I have a few months in Virginia before we move to Colorado, where he'll be stationed at Fort Carson in Colorado Springs. He has this weekend off from quartermaster school, and he wants to take me for a drive to explore the area. He books a hotel in Washington, DC, and after we check in, he tells me there's a restaurant nearby where we can get dinner. It's dark out as we walk past the White House, but the place is all lit up. It's beautiful. Even though I'm still pretty anxious about moving—and about the baby—this moment is nice. Out of the corner of my eye, I see that Brent has bent down to get something. I turn to him and see that he isn't bending down. He's on one knee, facing me.

I look into his face and my eyes are wide—they probably

look like they're about to pop out of their sockets. *What is he doing?*

"Emily," he says, "I love you. Will you marry me?"

Did Brent just say what I think he said? Is he serious? Does he know me—know that I fail at everything? Know that I ruin everything? Does he know all the problems I've had in the past and that every time, it was my fault?

I want to say yes, but I have to be sure. *This wonderful man wants to marry me? Emily?*

"Really? Are you sure?"

Brent looks at me like I'm crazy. "Of course I'm sure!"

I manage to blurt out, "Okay, then. Yeah! Let's get married."

Brent stands up and puts a ring on my finger. We kiss and he grabs my hand. We're swinging hands, walking to the restaurant. I feel like I'm floating on air. *Is this real?*

I ask Brent, "For real? Like for *really* real?"

He laughs and says, "Yes! Yes, yes, YES!"

I'm surprised, but I'm worried too. I cannot fail at this. It's too big—too important. At dinner, I talk to Brent about my misgivings.

"Listen," I say. "If we really are going to get married, that's it. I'm not going to have a kid and then get divorced. If you're sure, then okay. But if you're not 100 percent positive, then we should slow down so you can think about it more."

Brent looks me in the eye. "Yes, Emily, I'm sure. I'm positive. I want to marry you, and we are not getting divorced. Now let's celebrate being engaged, okay?"

He's smiling, and now I'm smiling too. I love this man.

* * *

The shock is wearing off, and after a week, I'm glowing. We're really going to do this. Now that it's certain, I don't want to wait another minute to be married to Brent. We talk about a wedding, but it's the second time around for us both, and neither of us really wants to go through the whole ordeal of a traditional wedding again. We just want to be married. Brent suggests eloping, and I reluctantly agree. As eager as I am, I'm worried about upsetting my friends, especially Jill, Kim, and Sarah. They've stood by me for so long, and it's not like me to leave them out of anything.

"Let's get married tomorrow," Brent says. I can tell by the look on his face that he's serious. *Tomorrow.*

I hesitate, but for just a few seconds. Then, "Let's do it!" I say. *Am I really doing this? Yes, I really am. I want this. I want this so much.*

I have to start telling people: my family, my work family, and my friends. I start with Jill, the closest person to a mom I've ever known. I haven't called her in a couple of weeks, not since I got back from my trip to DC with Brent. I had told her then that I was engaged. She probably doesn't think I'd be getting married this soon, and I wonder how she'll respond.

I take a deep breath. I'm a little worried, but I have to do this. I call Jill and she answers immediately. Her bright voice reassures me.

"Hey, Mom," I say, "Guess what! Brent and I are getting married tomorrow."

"Why are you rushing?" she asks. "Are you pregnant?"

Jill doesn't sound happy for me; she sounds angry. When I don't respond, she hangs up. I'm sad, but I don't call her back. I don't know what I'd say. I'm relieved when she calls me back a couple of hours later. I guess she's had time to think. The anger is gone from her voice, but she sounds hurt—like she's disappointed or something.

"I'm sorry, Emily," she says. "I just thought you would have told me sooner. This is a big deal. And I'm upset that you're not going to have a wedding too."

That makes me feel bad. Maybe I should have told Jill sooner. I probably should have told my daddy and my brothers, too, and Kim and my other friends. But I've been afraid of what they might think of me, and how being married, being pregnant, and having a baby is going to change our relationships. I don't want them to judge me. I don't want them to *abandon* me.

But now I realize that people who care about me like Jill does won't judge me. They just want to be invited into my joy. They want to celebrate along with me. I never thought about it that way until now.

I call my daddy, and he isn't upset at all. What a relief.

Brent and I get married. It's a quick ceremony, and afterward—even without the gown, or the church, or the big reception—I feel different. Like I have a partner in this life. It's a good feeling.

* * *

It's time to break the news about my pregnancy to my daddy. I'm so nervous, but I don't want to do this over the phone. I need to see him in person. This is big news, even bigger than getting married.

I don't want to hurt my daddy. He's a religious man, and he's not stupid. He knows that Brent and I planned to elope, and when I tell him when our baby is due, he'll know what's up. I might as well just say, "I found out I'm pregnant, and that's why we decided to get married so quickly." I'm sure that would go over well.

Daddy and Mary live in Wisconsin now. They moved there after he retired so Mary could be closer to her family. I fly to Wisconsin to give him the news. I can't do this over the phone. I know he'll be disappointed in me, and the least I can do is give him the chance to tell me how badly I messed up. I have it coming.

"Hey, Daddy," I say, "Brent and I are married. That's what I came here to tell you." Then I hand him a framed photo—the ultrasound picture. "And congratulations, you're going to be a grandpa."

I hold my breath, waiting for the disappointment, the judgment, the sadness. Instead, Daddy hugs me so tightly I can hardly breathe. When he lets go, I can see the tears in his eyes. He's so happy and excited, he's almost crying. He takes off his glasses and wipes his eyes, then he holds the photo up for a closer look. He's smiling from ear to ear.

My father is proud of me for getting married, and he's thrilled that Brent and I are starting a family. He wants grandkids—has been talking about it for years—and I'm the first one in the family to make it happen for him. His approval is like the icing on the cake. I don't ever want to disappoint my daddy.

Mary, my stepmom, laughs. "I should have known by the shirt you're wearing," she says. She's right. I have a baggy shirt on to cover my growing belly. Mary isn't making fun of me though—she's just as excited as my daddy.

"Do you know if it's a boy or a girl?" she asks.

I shake my head.

"Well, let me know as soon as you know," she says. "I'm going to make him or her a blanket."

After enjoying a few days in Wisconsin with Daddy and Mary, I fly back to Virginia. The tough part's over—telling Daddy—so it's time to call my brothers and give them the news.

Andrew's in New York, and as soon as I tell him I just got married, he says, "Why? Are you pregnant?"

I call Philip and he says the same thing.

Brothers!

CHAPTER 6

Mother Trauma

BACK IN VIRGINIA, I POST MY GOOD NEWS ON FACEBOOK. It's public, so Jennie sees it, and she messages me. I respond and the conversation continues, with me agreeing to pay her a visit with my new husband. We make a quick trip of it—out and back—and the best thing I can say about the day is that it's uneventful. In my family, especially when it comes to Jennie, uneventful is very good.

With Brent's schooling complete, he's off to Colorado to begin work, but he wants to find us a house too. I decide to go back to work at the restaurant for a while. I can stay with Kim, have a little more time with my friends before leaving Florida, and make a little money too.

I'm starting to show, and my friends throw me a baby shower. Brent's mother and sister are there, along with my friends from home and from the restaurant. This is starting to feel real. I'm going to have a baby. I'm going to be a mom.

* * *

I like being around my friends, and even though I'm eager to be with Brent, I stay at Kim's house in Florida until I'm thirty-four weeks pregnant. But now it's time to go. Kim and I spend hours loading up the truck. It's a big Silverado that Brent bought when we were together in Virginia, and I'm glad he left it behind for me. I have just over a month before my due date when I start the cross-country drive to Colorado.

My first stop is Jacksonville, where my brother Philip now lives. Andrew flies in from New York, and Daddy flies in from Wisconsin. We'll all have Thanksgiving together, then my daddy is going to share the driving with me to Colorado. The thought of driving in snow makes me nervous, and I tell Daddy that whenever we see snow, he's driving!

Maybe I should be nervous about everything else, but I'm not. Everything is about to change, but I'm not nervous—I'm excited. I want this.

Brent and I have never really lived together, outside of sharing a hotel room in Virginia. Now I'll be living in a house with him. I've been working for years at the restaurant and as a Body Glove model, and I'm giving all that up to rely on him for money. I'm also moving to a state I've never lived in and have visited exactly one time: to check out the house. Maybe I'm crazy, but none of that bothers me. I'm happy, so happy, and Brent is the reason. He will be there to welcome me to a new state and a new home. He'll provide for us, so I won't have to worry about working. I don't know when I've ever felt so safe and secure. So sure about something. I'm sure about Brent.

* * *

Daddy and I arrive in Colorado at night. I can see snow on the ground, but it looks like it's melting, and the roads are dry.

Daddy stays the next day, then we take him to the airport so he can fly back to Mary.

I have a lot of unpacking to do. Between sorting through boxes, I text my friends back home in Florida. Brent's at work all day, and aside from grocery shopping and doctor's appointments, I have nowhere to go and no one to see. I'm not used to all the "alone time," and I like it. With so few responsibilities, I take it easy for a change. When I get bored, I text Kim, Sarah, Jill, and my other friends. Or I watch *Game of Thrones* and eat Goldfish crackers right out of the box. Sometimes, I message Jennie on Facebook.

Everyone wants to visit me in Colorado after the baby's born, and Jennie's no exception. I'm open to that—I want it, in fact. I've let go of the possibility that she'll ever explain why she left my brothers and me years ago. I don't expect an apology. I want to move forward now, and I want Jennie in my baby's life. Jill has already made it clear that the little one will be calling her "Grandma," but I still want the baby to know its biological grandmother. This seems like the best way to begin mending the damage between Jennie and me and to get our relationship back on track. After all, babies are so wonderful, so sweet. I already love my baby, even though I haven't seen it yet, and I know Jennie will too.

My daddy, Brent's parents, Jill, and Sarah will be out for the birth or right after, to see the baby. Jill is in the delivery room when Zechariah is born. When she cuts the umbilical cord, I know that she's not only my "forever mom," but she's my newborn son's forever grandma too.

After a couple of weeks, everyone leaves, and it's just me alone with the baby during the day. Brent had just ten days off from work, so now he's gone all day, but he's home with us every night, usually after dark. These few weeks with the three of us together are a special time. It's not perfect though, because I develop mastitis from breastfeeding, which is very painful. The doctor gives me antibiotics to fight off any infection, but it still hurts so much to feed my baby. I push through the pain, but I'm not getting enough sleep. I'm tired all the time.

Zechariah's eight weeks old now, and Jennie's coming to stay with us awhile so I don't have to be alone all day. This way, we can get to know each other again, and maybe with her here to help with the baby, I'll be able to get some sleep. Everyone warned me about how tired I'd be. Jennie will be a big help. I'm glad she's coming.

* * *

Jennie's here today, and I'm so hopeful that everything will work out. She's unpacking her things: clothes, toiletries, and... *What's that?* Three gallon-size Ziploc bags full of prescription bottles!

"Whoa," I say, "That's a lot of pills." I don't mean to sound so judgmental, but come on! I thought that after all this time, Jennie had gotten herself together. *What is going on?*

Jennie tells me it's all pain medication, but when she starts to explain what each one is for, I have to walk away. I don't believe her. There is no way she needs all these pain meds! *She hasn't changed at all*, I'm thinking. *What did I just get myself into?*

I'm afraid to leave her alone with Zechariah, but Brent wants to give her a chance. He wants me to trust her a little bit and see how everything plays out before I assume the worst, which is what I'm doing. But I know Jennie. I know her all too well. I just thought she had changed. Brent reminds me that she's our baby's biological grandmother, after all, and she seems normal enough to him. He presses me to leave Zechariah with her one evening so we can go on a dinner date.

I give in, and we go out for a quick meal. Any new mom knows how hard it is to separate from their baby, especially for the first time, and my anxiety is heightened by my worry about Jennie. After forty-five minutes, I have to get home.

I hear Zechariah crying the minute I get in the door. Jennie's rocking him, and she has a stressed-out look on her face.

"He screamed and cried the whole time you were gone," she says in a complaining voice, as if it's my fault that her day has been ruined by my screaming baby. Zechariah is colicky and he does cry often, but he never screams, so I hope she's just exaggerating.

Jennie makes a big deal out of it, and I feel bad—guilty even, for leaving her alone with my baby. I can't change my emotions, and the guilt is real. But intellectually, in my thinking mind, I'm trying to figure out her behavior, and it isn't meshing with what I would expect from a grandmother. *Babies cry, and grandmothers deal with it, just like moms deal with it. Instead of making it sound like Zechariah is a huge inconvenience, shouldn't she be calming him and calming me, making us both feel reassured and at ease? Yes*, I answer myself, *but you know that's not how Jennie works.*

I don't leave her alone with Zechariah again.

* * *

Brent still thinks we should try to make the most of Jennie's time with us, so when she offers to take the baby in the mornings after I breastfeed him, I agree. I'm finally over the mastitis, but Zech's been waking up nearly every hour around the clock. I am so sleep-deprived. I would do almost anything for some rest.

"It doesn't matter how early, just bring him down," Jennie says, "This way, you can get a couple more hours of sleep." Sleep sounds great to me.

In the morning, we give it a try. I feed Zechariah and Brent takes him to Jennie. I fall into a deep sleep, still exhausted from giving birth and from taking care of my newborn most of my waking hours. This is just what it's like to be a new mom, and even though everyone warned me, it's not possible to understand what "tired" really feels like until you've experienced it yourself. Those extra hours of sleep are a godsend, and I wake up thinking, *Wow, this is going to be great.*

I head into the kitchen. Jennie starts in immediately.

"Brent came downstairs and woke me up!" she says, "He just gave me the baby and left, and I was barely awake."

"Oh, really?" I say, because that does not sound at all like something Brent would do. *Maybe something was going on with him? Did he have an early meeting or something?* I don't want to get into it with Jennie, so I apologize.

When Brent gets home from work, I ask him about what happened that morning. Brent's version is completely different from Jennie's.

"She was sitting up in bed with her glasses on and her laptop open, and when she was done typing, she put it aside and took the baby. She was wide awake, Emily. I even brought her a cup of coffee before I went to work." He sounds defensive, and I press him for details. Their stories don't match.

We're sort of bickering now, and I stop suddenly and say, "Brent, let's not do this. I've told you before that Jennie is a pathological liar. I don't trust anything she says, and you shouldn't either."

"But why would she say something like this? Tell you that she wasn't awake? It doesn't make sense."

He's right; it doesn't. That's Jennie.

"This is what she does," I tell him. "She enjoys the fighting. She wants to hear us screaming at each other. Sometimes I think she gets off on it. But we can't allow her to do this to us."

I now know that inviting Jennie into my home, my family, my life, was a bad decision. Between the pills, the lying, and now causing arguments between Brent and me, on top of the stress of being brand-new parents, we're ready for her to go. I can't trust her to be alone with Zechariah, and I can't even trust her alone with Brent. I have no idea what she might say to upset him or create friction between the two of us. And I can't say anything about her behavior because she will never accept responsibility for anything—she'd rather put me on a guilt trip, making it seem like everything that goes wrong is my fault.

I don't see this getting better—in fact, it could get much worse. What if she accidentally takes too many pain meds or combines them and there's a bad effect? What if she tells Brent more lies and tries to turn him against me? I know he's too smart to fall for that, but the drama she creates has no place in my home.

I'm worried for Zechariah. I don't want him growing up in a home with this person. I never thought I could love anyone as much as I love my husband, but with my baby, it's different— more intense. I don't just love him; I have an overwhelming need to protect him.

This is what it feels like to be a mother, I think, *a real mother*. Not like Jennie, but a mother who would lay down her life for her child. Part of me is relieved to have this feeling because it proves that I'm not like her and my baby will never feel the way that I did as a child. Another part of me is saying that the best way to protect my baby is to keep myself and my family away from Jennie.

This is how it'll have to be. I want Zechariah to know his biological grandmother, and I'm still willing to try to make things right between Jennie and me. But for now, I have to take care of my baby. My dream of a normal mother-daughter relationship, and a normal grandmother-grandson relationship, will have to be put on hold.

* * *

Around the same time that Jennie's leaving, Brent's military job is taking him to Kentucky for three months. Rather than stay in Colorado and take care of Zechariah by myself, I decide to go to Florida, where I can stay with Jill and be around my friends. Jennie's going with me so we can share driving time and she can visit her mother and sisters in Florida.

It's a long drive, especially for a baby. Passing through Atlanta, Zechariah is fussy and he's crying. He probably just wants to get out of his car seat, and I don't blame him. I just want to get through Atlanta and find a decent, affordable motel.

Now he's screaming, and I can tell he's hungry. I pull into the next motel along the road, and we check in. Walking to our room, I notice a couple of prostitutes hanging out, and I hope this isn't *that* kind of motel. Our room isn't just dirty; it's a mess. The bed's unmade and the trashcans are full. Whoever was here last left towels on the floor and leftovers in the mini-fridge. I try to call the front desk to let them know our room hasn't been cleaned, but the phone doesn't work. As much as I want to get Zechariah fed and let him sleep, we cannot stay here. Jennie and I turn tail and load our bags back into the truck, and I drive to the lobby to ask for a refund. I figure it's only been a few minutes since we checked in; surely, they'll give me my money back.

Nope. The guy behind the desk says, "No refunds. If you don't like the room, that's your problem."

I walk out and back to the truck. I'm not going to argue. Right now, I just need to find another motel.

When I tell Jennie they wouldn't refund my money, she gets angry.

"It's no big deal," I tell her, "I'll cancel the payment. Let's just find another place before it gets any later."

Jennie whips open the truck door and marches into the lobby. I can hear her loud and clear from the truck's cab. She's screaming obscenities and racist remarks at the man, calling him names, her hands waving in the air like she's having a total fit. She gets back in the truck and slams the door. I can't believe she did this, but at least it wasn't in front of the baby.

It's the same old Jennie, I think. *She hasn't changed one bit. She put up a pretty good act at the house, but now she's going to let it all out and be herself.*

One more state to go. I can do this. But after that, I'm putting a lot of distance between this woman and me.

* * *

We're finally in Florida. Jennie's eager to see her family, so we go to her sister Maggie's house. Everyone is there—my grandmother, all my aunts, their kids (who are my cousins), and my cousins' kids. It's a full house, and we're all in the living room. Jennie has Zechariah on her lap, and I'm sitting on the couch across from them. My cousin Trevor sits down next to me, and within minutes, he and Jennie are going at it.

Just like when I was a kid, I think. When other kids came to my house, and even when I was a teenager and boyfriends visited and this happened, they'd ask me why my family was always fighting. I'd say, "It's because we're Italian." That seemed like as good an explanation as any. I'd also tell them, "We're not fighting. My family just talks loud."

Sitting here now as an adult, I realize that isn't true. It was never true. This isn't talking—it's fighting.

Jennie leans forward and slides to the edge of her seat, her arms wrapped around Zech. She looks directly at Trevor and starts screaming and cussing. My cousin yells right back, and poor Zechariah looks around, eyes wide, as if to say, "Get me out of here."

He's just a baby, but I know that look. He's afraid, and I'm afraid too. This is the same fear I lived with as a child. Zech isn't safe in Jennie's arms, just like I was never safe in her arms. I stand up and take him from her, and without a word, we're out the door. I'm not doing this again, and I'm not subjecting my baby to it—ever.

No one calls after me. They just keep yelling at each other. No one calls or texts me either, to see if I'm okay. They simply don't care. Just like always. Nothing has changed.

I drive away, talking to Zech in low, calming tones. I want to take away what just happened. I don't want my baby going through what I went through, the constant fighting and cussing and shaming and guilt. I don't want him to get used to it, make excuses for it, or think for one minute that this behavior is normal. I don't ever want my baby to feel the pain that I felt, that I still feel. My face is wet with tears, and I brush them away with my hand.

I think about all the years I spent living with Jennie. They were traumatic. *Mother trauma.* Yes, that's exactly what it was, but it ends now. *There will be no more mother trauma, and no grandmother trauma for my little boy.*

I look at Zechariah, and he's staring at me with his little baby face. He's so tiny. I have to protect him. *Don't worry, little guy,* I say, *I'll take care of you. We won't ever go back there again.*

I roll down the truck's window and take in deep, slow breaths of air—in and out, in and out—to calm myself down. We need to go someplace else, someplace safe. I drive to Jill's.

CHAPTER 7

Depression

JILL'S HOUSE IS EXACTLY WHAT I NEED. IT'S A REFUGE
for me, and Zechariah thrives there. Jill puts him in the stroller
and takes him for walks around the neighborhood with her
dogs. Indoors, she lies him on his back on a mat that has dan-
gling toys for him to play with and a toy piano at the bottom
that plays musical notes when he kicks his feet. She sits on
the floor next to him and plays, and she loves reading books
to him too. Jill has a calm, nurturing vibe, especially around
Zech. I feel completely at peace here, a place filled with unconditional love.

As relaxing as it is to have Jill's help with my baby, being a
new mom is still difficult. Zech wakes up every hour through-
out the night. It seems that I no sooner get him back to sleep,
when he's awake again, and so am I. After a mere forty minutes
of rest, being woken up makes me miserable. I'm exhausted,
and it's not getting any better. Zech's colicky, and his naps are
too short. Unless we're feeding or entertaining him, the crying
and fussing are nearly constant.

I don't know how much longer I can do this. I feel like I'm

losing my mind. Desperate for help, I call Brent. I hate bothering him, but I can't help it. I'm crying as I tell him, "I'm sorry, but I'm so tired, and I feel like I'm going crazy." I am tired. I'm frustrated, too, and just...sad. So sad. Like I'm sinking deeper and deeper into a sadness that I will never come out of. I need someone to save me, someone to listen. Now I'm yelling.

Brent can barely understand me, I'm crying so hard. And I'm so loud. I can hear myself screaming into the phone, but I can't stop. *I'm tired, and I need sleep, and it isn't fair that he gets to sleep all night. I feel like a single parent. This isn't what I signed up for!*

I don't think he gets it though. He probably just thinks I'm a typical tired new mom. But this doesn't feel typical. It feels awful, and I'm scared.

* * *

Zech's been especially fussy today. I'm here alone with him, and it's been weeks since I had any real sleep. I feel like I'm losing it. Jill walks in from work, and I hand her Zech. She takes him, like she always does. Then I fall apart. I'm crying, yelling, and not making any sense, but I just can't hold it together anymore. Jill looks at me, trying to understand, but I don't have the words to express what I need to say. I have to get out of here.

"I have to leave!" I scream, and I'm out the door. I get in the truck, drive to the park down the road—too tired to drive any further—and bawl my eyes out. I'm crying so hard, I'm shaking all over. *What is wrong with me? What's wrong with my baby? Why won't he sleep? Why can't I deal with it?* I feel like such a bad mom. I want to be like Jill, not like Jennie, but I keep finding myself raising my voice around my baby. I don't want to be that kind of mom, and I don't want Zech to see me this way.

After a while, the sobbing stops and I collect myself. *Deep breaths.* I find a napkin in the glove box and look in the mirror, wiping my tears away. I hate how I look right now. Tired. Red-faced. I have dark circles under my eyes, and I feel like I've aged ten years since having the baby. *Deep breaths. Drive.*

I'm a little embarrassed when I get back to the house, but I know I won't be judged—that it's safe to go back. Jill has Zech wrapped in a big towel and she's drying his little head. He looks at me and smiles, and I try to smile back. "I fed him and gave him a bath, okay?" she says.

I nod. Of course it's okay. Jill cares for my baby the way I want to care for him, and I'm so grateful he has this woman in his life right now. She looks at me, really looks at me, and says, "Emily, what's going on? Is there anything at all that I can do for you?" Her voice is so kind and loving, like she really means it. Because she does. She loves me unconditionally when I'm happy and when I'm like this. She loves me like a real mom. Standing here right now in front of her, I feel like her daughter. I feel like I'm home.

"I want to be like you, Jill, like the mother you are. I don't want to be like the mother I had. And I'm trying so hard. But sometimes, I can't do it. And I want to learn."

Jill sets Zech down on the floor and wraps her arms around me. This is what I need, all that I need right now. This, and sleep.

* * *

After six weeks at Jill's, I fly to Kentucky to stay with Brent for a month. Zechariah's five months old and still not sleeping well, and neither am I. There has to be a solution. Brent, seeing me face to face, can see how this is affecting me. He researches something called the Sleep Sense program, which recommends letting babies "cry it out." I don't know if I can do this by myself, and Brent wants to help. Together we "sleep train" Zech, and I can't believe it—we're getting three to four hours of undisturbed sleep every night!

This is better than before. I felt like I was falling off a cliff and someone grabbed me and pulled me up. But I'm still tired most of the time, and feeling kind of numb. Zech's awake most of the day and still fussy. I'm not sad, but I'm not happy either. It's as if all my emotions have been washed away.

* * *

It's been a couple of weeks since we all got back to Colorado, and it feels good to be home. I like laying Zechariah down in his own crib. I like lying in my own bed to sleep. I like that Brent's here too. We're a family, but it seems we never get enough time together under one roof. This is nice. It's a relief.

Everything should be better now, and it is, sort of, except I'm still tired. I'm tired all the time. *Really* tired. The baby still cries a lot, and I cry too. Despite Jill's kind words and Brent's support, I still feel like a bad mom. Babies aren't supposed to cry this much. Moms aren't supposed to cry this much either. I'm supposed to be able to handle this. I don't know what's wrong with him, but I wish I could make it stop. He cries and I cry. I'm so tired.

I'm alone with Zechariah most of the time. I hold him and feed him and keep him clean. I clean the house too. And not just light cleaning—it's spotless. Housework is the one thing I can do right. It gives me a purpose and keeps my mind busy. I forget that I'm tired for a while—forget that the baby's crying and I'm a bad mom. The doctor says there's nothing wrong with Zech. Babies cry, and some babies cry a lot. I don't tell him that I cry too.

The house is sparkling, and maybe that makes up for all the things I can't do right. The toilets are scrubbed, the counters are wiped down. The laundry is clean and folded with all the wrinkles smoothed out, the edges lined up and matched just right. I put the clothes on hangers in the closet in perfect order—all facing the same way, all evenly spaced. Everything looks so good, so right. Nothing wrong here. Nothing to see, nothing to worry about. Just a perfect mom, a perfect wife, doing everything right.

Except that I'm not right. There's something wrong with me, and it's not going away. It's getting worse. I scrub and clean and sweep and wipe, and everything looks so good, but I'm still a mess inside. Those feelings from the past are coming back, and I want to hurt myself, to let out the pain. No, more than that. I want to make sure that whatever's wrong doesn't come out and ruin my beautiful home, my family.

What if I'm like her? Why wouldn't I be? Just like her and getting more like her every day. I could ruin everything unless I find a way to stop it. I've gone from tired, to numb, to spiraling out of control, but no one knows. No one sees. I go through the motions, smiling when people expect me to smile, telling everyone I'm alright. Keeping the house in tip-top shape. *Nothing to see here.*

* * *

There's one way to make this all go away. I don't know why I didn't think of it before. It's a simple solution that will end all the tiredness, the numbness, and the craziness in my head. No more pretending. No more smiling. Just rest.

I have a Glock 45. It's small and black, and I know how to use it. It would be fast and painless. I could do it in the garage—don't want to make a mess in the house. Don't want to get blood all over the carpet. Someone will have to clean it up. *Brent? Someone else?*

Don't want to wake up the baby either. Don't want him to crawl out of his crib and find me like that. He won't understand that I did it for him. That he'll be better off without me. I'm turning into a monster, and I don't know how to stop it. But if I do this, I don't know what will happen to him, and I can't make a plan. I can't ask someone to please hold my baby while I go in the garage and shoot myself in the head.

I'll wait. I need to think it through because I can't just leave him behind. That's what she would do—what she did. She left us all behind. She didn't love us enough to stay, but I love my baby, and I love my husband. I need to figure this out.

I'm going to clean the kitchen again.

* * *

"There's something wrong with me."

It's late when I walk into the kitchen. Brent doesn't even look up. He's home from work, and he's had a long day, and he's used to me crying and complaining, sometimes yelling. He knows being a mom is hard. He knows I'm tired. I tell him every day. This time, it's different and he has to listen. He has to see me, hear me. He has to do something. I need help. I say it out loud, for the first time ever.

"I need help."

I wipe my eyes with my pajama sleeve. I can't see Brent's face. It's dark, his head's down, and he hasn't spoken, so I continue.

"I'm severely depressed, Brent. That's why I've been so irritable and arguing with you about stupid stuff. And I'm sorry for that, but I feel like I can't help it. I can't make it stop, and I *need your help.*"

I'm crying again, covering my face with my hands. "I don't know what to do."

His arms are around me, holding me. "It's okay," he says. "I'll take care of you. I'm going to get you some help, honey."

I'm so relieved that I finally said it out loud—and that he actually heard me. His shoulders have lost some of that tense feeling, and I feel as if, for the first time, we're in this together. Like he understands this is serious and not something we can just shake off or fix on our own. Brent heard me, and he's going to help me.

I feel better already, just for acknowledging my depression and letting it out. It feels good to get rid of this weight I've been carrying around with me. My husband, the doctors, whoever we need is going to help me and I'm going to get through this. *We're* going to get through this. I've never asked for help before—didn't know how. I've never allowed myself to be this vulnerable. All my life, I've feared judgment, rejection, abandonment. I've had to be strong. I can't be strong all the time though, not when my family is at stake. Not when my *life* is at stake. I'm going to get help, and all I had to do was ask. *Ask the right person,* I correct myself in my head. *Ask someone who loves me.*

* * *

First thing in the morning, Brent's on the phone, calling doctors' offices on the army base. He doesn't want to waste another moment, and already I'm feeling different, like my life is about to change. He makes an afternoon appointment with a primary care physician.

Today, I think, *I'm seeing someone today.* This is unreal. A dream.

I don't want to go alone. Brent calls his boss to tell him that he won't be in today because I'm sick and he needs to take me to the doctor. I cringe when I hear this, but it's sort of true, and I'd rather he say that than spill all the details of my depression. I hold Zech on my lap on the drive to post, the army base, and Brent finds the medical office with no problem. We sit in the waiting room, and I'm still holding my baby and trying not to cry. It's a busy office, and there are lots of people around—patients waiting and nurses buzzing in and out of the room. People behind the reception desk too. I don't know any of them, and I don't want to cry in front of them, but it's hard to hold back the tears. I'm depressed, embarrassed, and afraid. *Was this a mistake?*

The nurse calls my name, and Brent takes little Zech from me, then he follows me and the nurse through a door and down a hallway. She takes my blood pressure and my weight, and now there's a questionnaire about depression. I have to answer on a scale of one to ten, the nurse says, and she asks each question out loud. I'm crying now, and so embarrassed to be in this situation. I've never felt so weak in my life, so weak that my husband had to rescue me. And now I'm sitting here like a fool, answering all these personal questions. *What does he think of me? How could he love me?*

"Have you ever wanted to hurt yourself?" she asks. I think about the cutting. I think about the Glock. My husband doesn't know about those things, *and he can never know,* but I answer honestly, *yes, number ten, I have thought of hurting myself.* If

I'm going to get help, I have to tell the truth. I can see Brent's face absorbing my answers, filing them away.

I'm so ashamed. I'm not the woman he thought I was, the woman he thought he married. I can't look at him or the nurse. I hang my head. I want to disappear. Behind the couch, into the tall grass. I want to be anywhere but here, but there's nowhere to hide. The nurse leaves, and Brent takes my hand. *Does it feel different? Or am I just imagining that? Does he still love me? Is he ashamed of me? What is he thinking?*

The wait is hard, just sitting there, crying softly and afraid to speak. But it's not long because the doctor comes in shortly. He's quick and to the point.

"Hi, Emily," he says. "You probably have postpartum depression. I'm going to write you a prescription for antidepressants and send you over to the psychology department to meet with a therapist there."

Then he's gone. He didn't ask me a single question. He didn't say that I would be okay either. There was no conversation at all. I thought he would want to understand me, talk to me a little about what's going on and why I'm here. I guess he just read my answers to the survey and decided I need pills and therapy. I'm not feeling good about this. Maybe asking for help and telling the truth about my depression really was a big mistake.

* * *

It's been a week since that visit with the doctor, and I've been taking the antidepressants every day. Today I'm at the therapist's office for my first appointment. I wish the therapist were a woman, but I didn't get to pick. The doctor assigned me to this man. *This is not a good match. How can this guy possibly know what it feels like to have a baby and be tired all the time, and have postpartum depression?*

I feel embarrassed and uncomfortable because I don't like talking about my feelings, and I don't want to think about what led me to be so depressed. My family never talked about problems; we just pushed them aside and kept moving forward. Now I have to sit in this office with a stranger and tell him everything.

I start with the obvious: having a child and not getting enough sleep. But then I open up and tell him more. *That's what I have to do, right?* I explain to him that what added to my sadness was losing my independence—moving away from my friends and family, living with my new husband, having to ask him for money for groceries when I was used to making my own way. I feel like I've lost everything I've ever known, everything I've built for myself as an adult. I had all this control over my life, and now it's all gone. *All I have control over these days is the laundry, the dishes, and housework,* I think.

The therapist looks me in the eye. He has a kind face, and I feel like he's hearing me. *This is it...This is the help I need.*

"You know, Emily," he says, "a lot of people would feel blessed to be in your situation."

He goes on to tell me how lucky I am to have a family and not have to work or worry about finances. How lucky I am that Brent has a great military career and all I have to do is stay home and be a mom. He's trying to placate me, and he's so patronizing I want to scream.

I go to one more session, but that's it. This guy is not making me better—he's making me worse. Now I feel guiltier than ever for being depressed. I am apparently a huge burden on my husband. An ungrateful mess of a woman who just doesn't know how good she has it.

I'm not giving up though. I tell Brent it's not working, that I can't connect with the therapist, and I don't want to see him anymore.

Brent isn't giving up either. "Let's find someone else then. If it's not working for you to see a doctor on post, we can pay out of pocket. We're going get you help, Emily."

I never noticed before that Brent always says *we*, like we're in this together.

* * *

The antidepressants have horrible side effects, worse than depression. Instead of feeling tired all the time, I'm all zingy and buzzy. My heart races, and it feels like everything is in overdrive. I can't sleep at night because I'm so amped up. I have diarrhea all the time, no matter what I eat, and even though it's the middle of winter, my armpits are drenched with torrential sweat.

I try—I really do—for eight weeks, but I can't keep taking them. I go back to the primary care physician who prescribed them and tell him, "These antidepressants aren't working for me. I need to try something different."

"That's the only option," he says.

I plead with him. "There *must* be something else I can take."

"No," he says. "I can't change your prescription. Sorry."

I can't believe this. How am I supposed to get better like this? I call my brother Philip. We don't talk often because we're both so busy. Over the years, he's gotten married and finished college. He and his wife are both nurses. I talk to him about the antidepressants, and he says there are other options, and my doctor should be able to discuss those with me. *So maybe I need a different doctor?* I don't know what to do, but I can't keep going like this. I stop taking the pills.

*　*　*

I'm pregnant. I didn't plan for this to happen so soon, but I'm happy about it. Brent and I have talked about having three kids and if not now, then when? I'm really glad I stopped taking the antidepressants when I did because I wouldn't want to be on medication and carrying a baby. The funny thing is that after I stopped taking the pills, my depression subsided. I don't cry so much anymore, and I'm less tired. Maybe it's the baby and the pregnancy hormones. I don't know, but it's nice to feel normal again.

Brent's thrilled that I'm pregnant. He's being so supportive too. It's a relief to be able to talk to him more, since going to the doctor and the therapist. He takes everything I say seriously. If I'm in a bad mood when he comes home from work, he talks to me. He wants to know what's going on and how he can help, and I don't feel so weird talking to him about my feelings anymore. The antidepressants and therapy didn't work out, but my marriage is much better. I can tell Brent anything now.

Being pregnant this time around, my body seems to have balanced itself out. I don't have any of those dark thoughts or feelings of depression. I'm not going back on medication and with Brent's support, I don't even want to see a new therapist now. I don't feel like I need one. Still, I have to make sure I'm okay.

I never would have thought I could say this to my husband, but today I tell him, "Brent, if you see any signs of depression in me after this baby is born, you have to let me know. I can't get that way again."

Learning to be vulnerable has been hard, but it's liberating too. I can let Brent see the worst of me and not worry that he's going to leave.

"You'll tell me, right?" I say, "Promise?"
He promises.

CHAPTER 8

Taking Control

BRENT'S GOING TO BE AWAY FOR TRAINING A LOT DURING
my pregnancy, and his unit is about to be deployed. I don't
want to be alone, so we rent a house in Florida where I can
stay for a while. It's just ten minutes away from Jill's, or Mom's,
because that's what I call her now. Brent's parents are an hour
away. I like having people who care about my son and me so
close by.

Being a mommy to Zech is my favorite role. We go to the
community pool, the playground, and Mom's house. Sometimes we just stay home. Zech likes to run around naked in his
kiddie pool, and I feed him cut-up fruit out of a bucket. Brent
FaceTimes with us every morning and night, and he flies out
to visit whenever he has time off. It's a good life.

Jennie's in town. Her sisters, my aunts, have been taking
care of their mom who's developed Alzheimer's and dementia.
They're going to put her in a place where she'll get full-time
medical care, and Jennie is here to help with that process. She
calls to ask if I can come by to see her at her mom's, my grandmother's house. I think about all the glass trinkets in that place

and decide it wouldn't be fun for me or Zech, so I ask her to come to my house instead.

I haven't seen Jennie since the day I took my baby from her arms at my aunt's house. Once in a while, I get a card or a care package for Zech from her. After all this time, I'm sure she'll come, but she doesn't. I wonder if I should feel guilty about this, like I'm being a bad daughter, but I know I shouldn't. I have a toddler and I'm pregnant, and I don't need any stress in my life. If she really wanted to see Zech and me, she'd come to us. The weeks pass, and even though she's just a few miles away, she never comes to visit.

* * *

I give birth to my little girl, Harper, in Florida. Brent has two weeks of leave, so he's here for the birth, and I'm so happy. I wish he could stay longer.

Harper's about six weeks old when Brent flies in again, this time just for the weekend. He kind of surprises me when he says, "I think you should talk to a doctor, Emily. You're starting to act a little different and being extra irritable, like you were after Zech was born."

Even though I'm taken aback and I haven't noticed the changes myself, I take his words seriously. I find a female primary care physician nearby, and she seems to know a lot about postpartum depression. Dr. Myer listens to me and seems interested in learning all about my symptoms. The more I talk to her, the more I realize that I have been feeling...off. Brent was right; I am slipping back into depression. The doctor explains the different types of antidepressants and their side effects. Then she chooses one and explains why she thinks it's the best choice for me. This time, the pills seem to work, and there are no weird side effects.

* * *

Brent's been away for a while, but he's coming to Florida this week to see the kids and me. I can't wait to see him. I'm grateful for the help I get from his parents and from Mom, but living alone with two babies is still a little rough. I'm looking forward to time with my husband.

An actual dinner date would be amazing, but no one's available this weekend to watch Harper and Zechariah. Jennie's around, I know. Jennie. I swore I'd never leave her alone with one of my kids, but I'm so desperate to just get out of the house and be an adult for a while, instead of just a mom.

I ask Brent, "What do you think about asking Jennie to come over for just two hours so you and I can go out to dinner?" I don't even know if she'll come, but maybe if she thinks I need her, like I'm asking her to do me a favor, she'll make an exception.

Brent actually agrees. "Sure," he says. "Give her a call."

"I don't want to go too far," I tell him. "Just a short evening out."

I call Jennie, and she sounds excited. *Huh.* "Yes, I'd love to!" she says. "I can't wait to spend time with the kids."

Maybe it's going to be fine.

I tell Zech that he's going to see Jennie, or *NeNe*, as he calls her, and he's thrilled. He hasn't seen his grandmother in a long time.

I go through my closet and pick out my most flattering outfit—not easy when you've just had a kid, but I do my best. I'll shower and do my hair, put on makeup. I can't believe how excited I am to be going out to dinner, but it's been so long! I can hardly wait.

An hour before Jennie's supposed to come over, her sister, my Aunt Debbie, calls.

"Emily? Your mom's not going to be able to make it. She thinks she has a kidney stone, so she's going to the emergency room. She's in a lot of pain."

I only wish I could believe her, but I don't. I know Jennie. I know how she lies and how she manipulates. And I've seen her bags of pain meds. She must have run out and made up a fake condition so she can go to the ER and get more. To add to the drama, she does it when she knows I'm waiting for her to come over and watch my kids. Classic Jennie.

I tell Zech and he's disappointed, and it sucks. This is not cool. *My little boy.* It's bad enough that Jennie jerks me around, but when she does it to my kids, I can't stand it.

I tell Brent too. "I'm so *pissed.* I don't know why I let myself think she would actually come spend time with her grandkids. She just blew them off because she needed more pills! This is what she does, but I'm done."

"I'm glad you're finally done," he tells me. *How long has he waited to say that?*

Maybe she did have a kidney stone. I don't know. It's hard to believe anything she says. But from now on, no more time with NeNe for my kids. I'm not putting them through that. They have Mom, my daddy and Mary, and Brent's parents, and they're all fantastic grandparents to my babies. I have to protect myself from Jennie and protect my kids too.

I'm cutting her out of my life. I don't need her, and my kids don't need her, and we're better off without her. I think about what my brother once said to me: "The fact that you're conscious every day of what you're doing already makes you a better mom than her."

I finally believe him.

* * *

I won't be in Florida forever, and keeping the kids from Jennie is starting to make me feel a little guilty. I decide to invite her to Zechariah's birthday party. There will be a lot of other people there, so if she doesn't show up, he won't be so upset about it. Brent flies in for the weekend, and Kim, Brent's family, and Mom and her husband, Russell, are here. I invite everyone I can think of, knowing that soon enough, I'll be heading to Colorado.

Jennie shows up late and walks around talking to everyone except me. She introduces herself as my mom to one of Brent's friends, who looks perplexed. I had introduced Jill as my mom to this person earlier. She looks at me, and Jennie looks at me, and I shake my head. I'm not having any drama today—not at my son's birthday party. Jennie doesn't press the issue, thankfully. She must notice that Zech is calling Jill "Grandma" too. I'm not apologizing though. This is the life I want and the people I want around me. It's my safe place, and Jennie can't ruin it for me.

She doesn't stay long.

* * *

A couple of weeks after Zech's birthday, we're back in Colorado. Harper's three months old now, and Brent will be out of the military soon. After that, we can go wherever we want. We've been talking about what comes next and decided we'll stay here for a while.

Even though all my friends are back in Florida, I need room to grow, and the sky feels higher here. I know that sounds silly, but that's how it feels. I'm not the same person I was in Florida. I've changed a lot, and I want to keep changing and growing. I'm getting my independence back and making decisions for myself. More than that, I'm becoming the wife, the mother, and the woman I want to be, and I don't want anything holding me back—not the places, the people, or the memories. There was so much bad before, and I need to get away from it and figure out who this person, this Emily, really is. I think I'm finally starting to find out, and I like her a lot. Every day, I like her more.

I still love my friends back in my hometown, still cherish many of the memories. But right now, I need this space. So I'll stay here in Colorado, and Brent, Zechariah, Harper, and I will be a family.

* * *

Brent's out of the military, and he started his own business. He's around a lot more than he used to be, and it's so nice not doing this on my own. We really are a family now, spending time together, having meals together, all sleeping in the same house for a change. Brent and I are parenting together, and we're learning how to do that the best way for the kids.

I'm helping him with the business, too, and that feels good. Being a mom has been a full-time job, but it's much different than building something outside the home. I hadn't worked in a long time, and I missed contributing in that way. Brent's been supporting me, and now I help support him and our family. We're in a good place, and I'm excited for the future.

It's time I got off the antidepressants. I've been on them since Harper was born, but everything's different now. I'm excited to give the news to my doctor, but she says it isn't a good time. I don't know why it isn't a good time because I feel great.

"Let's revisit this in the spring," she says.

That aggravates me. What difference does it make, now or

in the spring? It's winter, sure, but I'm ready. I don't say anything and pretend to go along with her decision, but secretly, I've decided to wean myself off the pills. I stop taking them on Sundays, then I cut back to five days a week. I haven't told anyone, not even Brent. I'm proud of myself, getting off these things. If I keep cutting back, I'll be off them completely by the spring.

Besides, it's almost time to start trying for another child. Harper's one, and we want to keep the kids close in age. I don't want to be on antidepressants when I get pregnant.

And just like that, I'm pregnant with our third child. It happened faster than I expected, but I'm happy, and Brent's happy too. Three kids—a family of five—is perfect. It's what we wanted. Plus, the business is going well, and I'm getting off the antidepressants. I'm glad I cut back, but I can't be taking them at all anymore. I quit cold turkey.

* * *

This pregnancy is different than the first two. I'm in the first trimester, when I'd usually be feeling great, but I'm sick all the time. Not just tired either but violently ill. My heart races, and I'm nauseous. I sweat profusely and have crazy mood swings. I don't know what's happening. I tell my brother about it. Philip's an emergency room nurse now, and when I tell him about the antidepressants, he says I shouldn't have gone off them all at once.

"You're going through withdrawal, and there's nothing you can do now but power through," he says. So I do, and I think I have morning sickness, too, because I feel awful, and it's been going on for months. I'm sick, and I'm pregnant, and I still have the kids and the house and trying to help with the business.

I'm getting those thoughts again—thoughts of hurting myself, of ending myself.

I'm a bad wife and a bad mother. I ruin everything, and I don't deserve to be here. Nobody cares about me, and they wouldn't even miss me if I disappeared, maybe went away forever.

My intellectual mind tells me these thoughts are all wrong, but I have no control over them. My emotional mind is taking over, making me feel undeserving of my husband, my kids, and my life. I feel...*worthless.*

This time, Brent sees the change in me right away. I don't even have to ask.

I'm in the kitchen and thinking maybe I should say something to him. I can't let this get away from me. Before I even speak, he says, "Emily, I can tell something's going on. Let's get you some help again."

He makes an appointment for me, this time with a female, Christian-based therapist. I haven't been to church in a long time, but Brent knows I grew up in a religious household, going to church every Sunday, and that I still hold to the Christian values I learned from that experience and from my father as a child. I start something called *talk therapy,* where the therapist and I have long conversations to get to the root of my depression. I wish I had done this years ago because it's incredibly helpful.

I tell the therapist, Patty, about my past depression, and about my childhood. I tell her about Jennie, too. She wants to know how I feel about Jennie now, and I tell her that I haven't forgiven her. Instead, I've pushed down all my feelings about her and focused on my life with Brent and the kids. The therapist encourages me to forgive Jennie, not for her sake but for my own. She says it's time for me to accept my biological mother for who she is—that I need to do this before I can truly move on in a healthy way.

This is what I needed. I needed to be heard and understood. I needed clear direction. I needed to be shown the way out of my past so I could embrace my present and my future. Brent has been so supportive all these years. Mom and my friends have stood by me. My kids love me so much. I always thought that should be enough. I felt so needy asking for more. But I wasn't acknowledging the mother trauma I had suffered for so many years and how it has affected me in my adult life. Talking to Patty, I have to be completely vulnerable. I tell her everything, and it's painful. Exhausting. But afterward, I feel lighter. I see everything more clearly, and I see the path ahead. It's bright, and it makes me smile. *Is this what it's like to be happy?* After all these years, I don't have to pretend anymore.

* * *

Choosing names for my first two children was difficult enough—I have no idea what I'm going to name this one. I look at Zech and Harper. Their names fit their personalities perfectly, and I chose them without even knowing who they were. I'm hoping I get lucky a third time, but where to start?

I turn to the internet and search for baby names. Zechariah is beside me, helping me out. I read each name aloud, and Zech vetoes them one by one. I'm already halfway through the alphabet—to the letter "o"—and feeling discouraged. One "z" child is enough. We need another letter.

"Oliver?"

"Nope," Zechariah shakes his head.

"Omar?"

"No, Mommy."

"Oscar? Otis?"

"No and no."

"Otto?'

"Yes!" he yells emphatically.

"Really? Otto? If Mommy has a boy, you want your little brother's name to be Otto?"

"Yes."

I have to think about this for a while, but the more I consider the name, the more I like it.

Our third child is a boy, and we name him Otto. The minute he's born, I know it's the right name. He looks just like a little Otto.

* * *

I'm worried about postpartum depression setting in, even though Brent says he'll pay attention and make sure he catches it before it's a problem. But this time, I'm fine. I don't go back on the antidepressants either because I don't need them. It must be the talk therapy.

I don't know how talking about myself for an hour every week can make such an amazing difference in how I feel, especially how I feel about myself, but it works. I'm learning about my feelings and where they come from, and I'm focusing on what the therapist calls my "internal dialogue." Patty is training me to change what I say about myself in my head. She's giving me a new internal dialogue to practice. I tell myself that "I am great." I say that "I'm a damn good mother and the best wife I can be." I say a lot of other things, too, all of them positive. This is working, and unlike the pills, there are no negative side effects.

We explore why I get to the point where I want to harm myself. Patty shows me that I don't actually want to harm my body; I'm trying to resolve an issue from my past, and I don't know how. The damage I do to myself comes from old, unreconciled pain. I have to revisit that pain to get to the root cause of my depression and heal it. For many years, I've been masking the symptoms of depression with antidepressants, instead of treating the sickness that's been festering in my head since childhood.

Among other issues, I have a fear of abandonment, which doesn't surprise me. When the one person in your life who's supposed to care for you and never leave you picks up and disappears, why wouldn't you have abandonment issues? My relationship with Jennie is the root cause of a lot of my problems, and it all comes out during talk therapy.

Besides uncovering the causes of my depression and other psychological issues, my therapist teaches me how to heal the damage. I learn not to be so hard on myself and that no matter what mistakes I've made in the past, I'm a good person and worth taking care of. I have value to myself and my family—great value, in fact. To my husband and children, I'm actually pretty wonderful.

I can't erase my past, but understanding how it's shaped my internal dialogue, personality, and behaviors empowers me to change those things. Not all of them, because most of them are good. I've just been focused on the bad stuff for so long that I couldn't even see all the good in myself. I don't have to live the bad parts anymore though—I can learn from them and consciously, intentionally change them. My biggest takeaway from the talk therapy is learning from the past—learning from the mother trauma—instead of living it.

Part of the healing is learning to show my emotions. I have strong emotions, but I've always covered them up. I learned at a young age that being emotional wasn't met with comfort. Often, it was met with ridicule, embarrassment, and pain. And as strong a front as I have put up for everyone as an adult, I'm an emotional person. To get healthy, I need to work on my relationships with the people I trust, and to do that, I have to show them my emotions.

This means more communication with people like Brent and Jill. It means being vulnerable. These people love me—in my conscious, intellectual mind, I know that. I have to train my emotional self to know that, too, and to trust them.

Brent and I start marriage counseling so we can learn to communicate better with one another. I'm reminded of how much he loves me and truly wants the best for me. He is here for me, unconditionally. He tells me so in the counseling, and even after being married all these years, even after having three children together, I tear up hearing him say that. I know he loves me, but there's something about hearing the words that makes it really real. Sometimes I just need to hear the words.

CHAPTER 9

The Seeds of Mother Trauma Were Planted Long Ago

PART OF FORGIVING MY BIOLOGICAL MOTHER, JENNIE, was understanding why she is the way she is. I don't believe people are born with a desire to grow up, have babies, and abandon them. I don't believe Jennie chose to be the woman she became, a woman who caused her daughter so much mother trauma. At some point in her adult life, she must have been aware of the pain she was causing and, for one reason or another, chose not to correct it. She chose not to seek help. She never saw her children as important enough for her to take action to protect them from, of all people, herself. She never saw *me* as important enough for her to learn to be a real mother.

They say a person's most important role model is their same-sex parent. So it's no wonder that whatever my de facto role model, Jennie, believed about me when I was a child, I believed too. And I kept believing it for many years: that I wasn't important, or useful, or good enough. That I wasn't worthy of love.

I wanted to know how Jennie became Jennie, so once I had truly committed to becoming the best mother I could be, I did some digging into my biological mother's family history. I didn't know exactly what I was looking for, but the goal was to examine the facts of Jennie's past without judgment, in an effort to understand her better. With understanding, I believed, would come forgiveness—my ability to forgive, or at the very least, calm the anger and the shame that had ruled my life for so long.

Unraveling the past helped me identify some of the threads that, woven together over time, created the imperfect tapestry that was my biological mother. In the process, I learned about generational trauma: trauma that's passed down from parent to child, and that, left unchecked, continues to be passed down for generations.

* * *

My maternal great-grandfather, James Ricci, was born in Italy in 1899. He moved to the United States in 1916 at the age of seventeen and became an auto mechanic in Lexington, Kentucky, where he met and married my great-grandmother, Margaret Plack, in the early 1920s. They had three children: James Alvin Ricci, Mary Lou Ricci, and my grandmother Ann Howard Ricci.

Margaret was a flapper. I didn't know what that meant, but my daddy told me that she was sort of a trouble-maker who went out a lot, slept around, and drank bathtub gin. She and James were both drinkers, and the marriage didn't last. James divorced her, left her and the children, and moved to Jefferson, Ohio, where he became a coal miner. He never made contact with them again, and Margaret was left to raise the three children on her own.

My grandmother Ann was just one year old when her father left. Her sister was five, and her brother was seven. Their mother wasn't around a lot, and when she was, she was drinking and yelling. My great-grandmother Margaret and grandmother Ann were constantly yelling at one another. Surprisingly, Ann didn't develop a drinking habit, so at least in that way, she wasn't like her parents. I remember only occasionally seeing her drink a beer.

The fighting between Margaret and Ann only grew worse as Ann became an adult, got married, and had children of her own. Margaret was always accusing Ann of stealing from her. One time, they fought for more than an hour over a suspected stolen hair comb.

During these fights, Ann's husband, my beloved Pop-pop, would go outside and hide in the shed or in the garage where he'd smoke cigarettes to calm his nerves. My daddy didn't smoke, but he dealt with Jennie the same way Pop-pop dealt with Ann: by removing himself from the chaos and waiting for it to subside. Pop-pop and my daddy wanted peace in their lives, but as long as they were married to Ann and her daughter Jennie, they would never find it.

* * *

My grandma Ann and Pop-pop were married on September 23, 1950, in Washington, DC. They lived in the DC area and Maryland for a while with their four children, three girls including my biological mother, Jennie, and a boy, Sean. My two aunts came first, then Sean, then Jennie.

When Jennie was sixteen, Sean was out with a friend of

his. His friend was driving a truck, and Sean was the passenger. They were hit by a drunk driver. The friend survived the crash, but Jennie's brother was thrown from the truck. He hit a concrete pillar and died immediately. Grandma, Pop-pop, and their three daughters were all deeply affected by the loss of Sean. I doubt if there was anything like grief counseling back then, and with Sean being Pop-pop's only son and Jennie's only brother, I can't imagine what losing him was like for them.

Jennie never talked about Sean to us when we were growing up. In fact, she never talked about her family at all, or what it was like for her growing up. I have to wonder whether her life with Ann was as miserable as mine with her.

Whenever her family got together as adults, there was constant yelling. Jennie, her mother, and her sisters fought loudly all the time. Holidays were a nightmare for us kids. On Thanksgiving and Christmas, we'd be excited for the meal and the gifts and the celebration, but getting together wouldn't be pleasant, and we knew it. If I took a boyfriend with me to Grandma and Pop-pop's, I'd warn them, before we even got out of the car, "Listen, when you go in there, it's going to sound like everyone's fighting, but they're not. That's just how my family communicates." At that time, I really did think that was how my family communicated—with raised voices. But it wasn't just the loudness; they were arguing, yelling, and fighting. They were speaking to each other, not with love and caring, the way families are supposed to interact, but with anger and fear and aggression.

* * *

I'm no longer in touch with anyone from Jennie's side of the family except for Katie, who's my favorite cousin. Katie was adopted, which makes me wonder if the mental and emotional instability I witnessed in Jennie and some of her family members is part of their genetic makeup. I know that some of them suffered from depression. That would certainly explain a lot.

* * *

Jennie and Daddy met when she was eighteen and he was twenty-eight. After a year of dating, they got married on May 15, 1982, in Vero Beach in Indian River County, Florida. That's where I grew up.

Jennie never lived on her own. She went from high school and living with Grandma and Pop-pop to making a home for my daddy. After three years of marriage, they had Andrew. Philip came along eighteen months later, and I was born eighteen months after him. We were glad to be so close in ages as kids because we went through the stages of childhood together and could relate to each other. I thought about that when I had my own children.

Growing up, I remember my daddy being gone most of the time—not because he didn't want to be around us kids but because he was always working. Daddy worked full time as a mechanic for the county, where he spent most of his time at landfill, road, and bridge construction sites, and he also had a part-time job at Walmart. Working sixty hours a week, plus the commute time and whatever breaks he got at work, left little time at home. Daddy wanted the best for us, and I guess he thought earning money was the best way he could do that. After I was born, he sold our little 900-square-foot home and used the money to build a bigger home. During that time, we lived with Grandma and Pop-pop for a while. I remember sleeping on a mattress on the floor in the room I shared with my brothers. That was a temporary situation, thankfully, and I was too young to really care anyway.

* * *

When I asked my daddy, as an adult, if he ever considered leaving Jennie for the safety of us children, he said, "My vows were for better or for worse." It wasn't until my biological mother cheated on him that he could convince himself to end the marriage.

I wish he and my Pop-pop would have been closer, but they weren't. They didn't dislike one another, but they didn't communicate much either. They were both dealing with similar issues though, and I guess they dealt with them the same way. Pop-pop stayed with Grandma until the end. Daddy stayed with Jennie until his faith gave him a legitimate out. Maybe they were two of a kind, and the women in their lives gravitated toward them naturally, knowing they'd put up with just about anything. Or maybe there was something engrained in these men as children that the women they married satisfied. I don't know.

* * *

I'm very proud of my two brothers and the men they have become. Like I said earlier, Philip's an emergency room nurse. Andrew's in school full time to become a nurse, and he works part time too. I don't think either one of them has a cruel bone in their body. Instead, they're good at helping people who need them. I think maybe they learned this as children, protecting one another and protecting me, their little sister.

Andrew's happily married. Philip is divorced, with one son,

and he's an amazing dad. He lives a few hours away, but we spend time together when we can, especially on birthdays and around the holidays. I love to see my own kids hanging out with their little cousin. During these get-togethers, there's no yelling, no fighting, and no drama. No mother trauma. My brothers have so much love to give their families and mine, and they do.

The way our families interact is so much different than the way we grew up. I can have my brothers and their families over to the house along with Brent's family, and everyone gets along. As kids, we either spent holidays with my daddy's family or Jennie's—never the two together. Despite all that happened back then, I sometimes feel like I'm the luckiest woman in the world, especially when my family and Brent's extended family all come together in one place. It's like a big, happy family—the kind of family you see in movies. The family I never in a million years ever thought I would have.

Sometimes Philip and I talk about what it was like growing up with Jennie. Andrew won't talk about it, and I don't press him. We've all had to learn to deal with our past in our own way, and I respect my brother's choice to put it behind him. For me, talking about it with someone who was there helps, so I'm grateful to Philip for listening, and also for confirming what I remember—especially when there are people on Jennie's side of the family who prefer to pretend that I'm remembering it all wrong. These days, they call that "gaslighting."

Working with a therapist helped me sort out a lot of what happened to me as a kid and helped me to better understand Jennie and her family. I gained some insight into why Jennie, her sisters, and their mother, Ann, behaved the way they did. And I'd be willing to bet that if I dug deeper and looked into how Ann's mother—my great-grandmother Margaret—was raised, I'd find a lot of similarities. That's how generational trauma works: it gets passed down from parent to child. And until a child finds a way to break that awful cycle, it continues through the future generations. For my children's sake, my husband's sake, and mostly, for my own sake, I knew I couldn't continue the cycle. I'm eternally grateful for finding Brent, my mom Jill, and my therapist, Patty. Without them, I don't know what my life would be like now. With their support, guidance, and mostly, their love, I put an end to mother trauma in my family, in this generation and the generations that follow. And when I look at Zechariah, Otto, and especially my daughter, Harper, I'm so glad I did.

CHAPTER 10

The Calm after the Storm

TALKING ABOUT INCIDENTS FROM MY PAST, EITHER WITH Philip, Daddy, Brent, or in talk therapy, was enlightening, and sometimes startling. I realized that what I often thought of as normal as a child and even into my teen years, I see in a very different light today. Looking back on them, not with an emotional mind but with my logical one, helps me break the emotional ties I had with those times so I can get past them and move on with my life.

For example, the time when I was four years old and I hid behind the couch, and Jennie said out loud to my cousin, knowing I could hear her, that she wished I'd run away. I didn't understand why she would say something like that back then, but now I think I do. Being hurtful was a way of life for her, and the closer a person was to her, the more pleasure she received from hurting them. I remember my cousin laughing, and now that I think about it, he was probably being treated similarly by his own mother. He may have experienced a great deal of pleasure seeing someone else being hurt for a change. Just understanding where their behavior came from and knowing that, really, I had nothing to do with it goes a long way toward helping that old pain go away. For years, I lived with an internal dialogue that told me "it's all my fault," when in reality, Jennie's cruelty wasn't my fault at all.

Having dish soap poured on my tongue wasn't my fault either. I still remember the taste of that awful stuff, and even now, as an adult, I never buy green dish soap.

Then there was the time when that man exposed himself to my friend and me at the soup kitchen. My biological mother was very angry about that, and I'm thankful that she and Daddy took the situation seriously enough to go to the police. But even though she didn't blame me, she never once said it wasn't my fault either. She didn't hug me or tell me that she loved me. She did nothing at all to comfort me. Today, looking at my own children, I can't imagine one of them going through something like that. But I do know that I would absolutely do everything in my power to make them feel comforted, and loved, and safe. And of course I would tell them that they did nothing at all to bring on that kind of behavior by another person. The idea of shaming my own children or making them feel guilty or responsible for someone else's bad behavior is beyond my comprehension. Healthy, normal people do not do that to the people they love.

After that incident at the soup kitchen, I only saw my friend Sheri one more time, at her birthday party. Something about our friendship had changed, and we felt kind of strange being around one another, so we stopped hanging out. When I spoke with Sheri years later, she mentioned it, too, like that terrible man who exposed himself had stolen something from us.

There are things about my brothers that I didn't understand

back then that I do now. Like, when we got spankings, why did Philip choose the belt or the paddle over the hand? What I didn't know back then was that between my two brothers and me, Philip was treated the worst by Jennie. I guess I never noticed it, but I learned this later from my daddy. Andrew was Jennie's first child, and when she became pregnant with her second, she really wanted a girl. Then Philip was born, and she wanted nothing to do with him. Even in the hospital, she refused to hold him. The nurses took care of him until she left the hospital. This behavior toward Philip continued, and he must have sensed it. Choosing the belt or paddle may have been his way of standing up to our biological mother, of sending the message "You can hurt me all you want, but you cannot break me. I'm stronger than you, tougher than you, and I'm going to survive you."

One thing I did notice, not when I was little but as a teen, was that Daddy favored Philip. In fact, Andrew and I used to get mad at Philip for being "Daddy's favorite." I learned later on that this was indeed the case. My daddy was trying to overcompensate for all the pain Jennie inflicted on Philip, by showing him extra love.

Jennie brought a lot of mental issues into our family, but some of her behavior may also be attributed to her situation. She never made a life of her own outside the home, at least not until she left us. Most of her women friends had careers, or at least jobs, but other than a few short stints as a cashier and clerk at Walmart and Uptons, Jennie was a stay-at-home mom. I think she resented my brothers and me for that. It must have eaten away at her self-esteem, hearing her friends talk about what they did at work, while all she had to talk about was housework and kids.

Jennie's prescription drug use didn't start out as recreational use that got out of control. She took the pills for pain after her old horseback riding accident injuries started acting up and never got off of them. Back then, this wasn't so common, or at least not so known. Today, we know that a lot of people get hooked on pain meds after an injury, especially opioids, and are unable to get off them.

When Jennie moved out of our home, she had been having multiple affairs. I didn't know that at the time. It started as chat room flirting and phone calls with strange men and evolved into meeting men at bars during the day when she told us she was going to the gym. I actually believed she was going to the gym to work out back then. If I had put two and two together, I probably wouldn't have been so surprised when she moved out or when Daddy finally decided to divorce her.

Jennie lied about a lot of things. I learned, later on, that she was never on a budget for groceries. My daddy gave her money for whatever she wanted. She had her own checkbook and used it to get her hair and nails done every week. I don't know why she told me, when I was a kid, that we were poor and that my daddy kept her on a strict budget. I didn't feel poor at the time and didn't understand. The truth is, we weren't poor. We were an average middle-class family. When Jennie talked badly about my daddy, it made me feel bad about myself. Maybe she knew that, and maybe she enjoyed it.

Jennie's cruelty showed up in a lot of different ways. Like the time she lopped off my hair. Harper has long, curly hair just like mine was at that age. She wears it up in pigtails or in a ponytail, and sometimes she likes to wear it down. She doesn't chew on it, but if she did, I would never, ever punish her by cutting it off. I would never do anything to humiliate my little girl. Remembering how I felt that day, sitting on that stool in the garage and bawling my eyes out, makes me feel very sad for that little girl I was. Sometimes I wish I could reach back in time and hug her, and tell her that she's beautiful, and that someday her life will be full of people who love her just as she is. People who don't care whether she chews on her hair. People who would never do anything to bring her harm.

Jennie's cruelty showed up in other ways, too, like how she always got rid of our pets. She'd wait until we had formed a connection with a dog, and then she'd make up an excuse to take it away. I've brought pets into my own household, but to me, taking in an animal is a serious commitment. The dog gets attached to the kids, and they to the dog. Just once, I did have to take a pet away, but only because it tried to bite Harper twice and did bite a boy who was visiting. The bite mark was superficial, and a Band-Aid and Tylenol was all that was needed to treat it, but I couldn't have a dog in the house that was biting kids—mine or anyone else's. We found a new home for that dog where it would be happier, and I talked to the kids about it so they wouldn't think they were—or the dog was—being punished or that they had done anything wrong. Today, our family dog, Josie, is Otto's best friend. When we moved from Colorado back to Florida and the kids asked, "Is Josie coming too?" I said, "Of course she is. She's part of the family, and we don't leave family behind."

* * *

So many episodes in my life can be attributed to depression. The running away and wanting to hurt myself. The cutting, the eating disorder, and the thoughts of suicide. As a teenager and even into my early twenties, I was never clinically diagnosed with depression, but in hindsight, my condition at that time is obvious. Especially in light of all that I've learned about myself as an adult.

I made so many mistakes back then and have many regrets. My rational mind is aware that I was a child and shouldn't be held accountable. When I look at my own children and consider their ages, I would never hold them responsible for similar errors in judgment. They're kids, for goodness' sake. Yet, my emotions have a mind of their own, and the shame I felt hiding behind that couch and in the closet, the embarrassment I experienced pulling a sweater over my scabbed arms or looking at my skeletal figure in the mirror still plagues me at times. Shame goes so deep, and it may be the hardest emotion of all to shake.

I know, intellectually, that all those behaviors can be explained based on my life at the time, my relationship with Jennie, and the depression. I know now that I had no real reason to be ashamed of any of it and that I shouldn't be ashamed. Still, those feelings linger. I can tell myself all day long how I should feel, but closing the gap between knowing how I should feel and truly believing it—absorbing it, accepting it, and abolishing that shame once and for all—alludes me.

The talk therapy helps. Being around people who see me a whole different way helps too. After all, if I'm such a terrible person, how could people as wonderful as my husband and my children love me so much? Thinking about them, I know I have good inside me. I know that they see it. And now, I believe it's there too.

* * *

I don't know if I realized it at the time, but Kim's friendship probably saved me from making some really bad decisions. If it weren't for her, I don't know if I would have stopped cutting myself. The funny thing is, I always felt like I was saving her—

as if, no matter how bad my life was, hers was worse, so I had to be there for her. In a way, I saw value in myself because of what I could do for her.

Kim helped save me from Seth, too, or at least gave me a safe place to stay while I was trying to save myself. Years later, Kim and her husband talked to me about my abusive relationship with Seth. The word "abusive" hadn't even entered my mind, but once it was out there, it was crystal clear to me that I had been abused, emotionally, verbally, and for a moment, physically. That was the first time I truly recognized what I had been through, and it was the first step toward letting go of the guilt I had been carrying around. It was the first step toward forgiving myself for something that wasn't my fault.

After my relationship with Seth ended, I researched his behavior to try and understand it. More importantly, I wanted to understand why I had put up with it. I came across the word "narcissist," and the definition fit Seth perfectly. Seth was a narcissist, and I, the devoted girlfriend who believed she didn't deserve any man, never mind a decent one, was the perfect target. I not only put up with his behavior, but I made excuses for it too. No matter how mean he was, I found a way to justify his behavior.

I think about the time we spent with the therapist. Up until then, Seth had controlled the narrative, and that therapist was taking the control away from him. I think that scared Seth. I believe he was worried that the therapist might open my eyes to what was really happening in our relationship and how Seth was controlling me. I wonder if Seth was afraid I would leave, if that was the real reason he stopped seeing the therapist. I suppose I'll never know what was going on inside his head.

I've thought about that relationship, and my place in it, a lot. How did I end up there? Now that the years have passed and I have some distance, both timewise and emotionally, I can clearly see the red flags that appeared early on. I ignored the red flags—the insensitive behavior and hurtful comments—and I stayed with Seth for the good times, which were so good. That meant putting up with the bad times, which gradually got worse and more common. I didn't see it happening in the moment. The pain, the oppression, the control that he had over me increased over time.

I was telling myself a story that wasn't true—a story of a good relationship that had a few problems. Just like I saw my relationship with Jennie—*she's my mother and she loves me. We just have a few problems.* I had gotten very good at rationalizing people's bad behavior over the years, even when it meant sacrificing my own happiness.

Thinking back now, I'm sure that, on top of all the abuse, Seth was seeing other women during our relationship. Maybe that's why he didn't want me to come back. I would be in the way.

I used to feel bad about that time in my life. It didn't help when people asked, "Why didn't you leave?" People who ask that question don't seem to understand how isolated I had become. How helpless I had allowed myself to become. Even when I wanted to leave, I was stuck, alone on the other side of the country and three thousand miles away from my friends, my family, my support system. I couldn't just grab a bag and drive across town to a friend's house. And I couldn't afford to get my own place. I worried about what leaving would be like too. I've learned since then that leaving is the most dangerous time for someone in an abusive relationship, and it did feel dangerous. I was terrified. Leaving would take planning, and more than that, it would take finding the courage to admit I had screwed up my life, and now I had to leave that life behind.

People who ask, "Why didn't you leave?" also don't understand how hard it is to leave a man you love, even when that man turns on you. Seth didn't turn on me all of a sudden, but with occasional words, small actions, and behaviors so minor that I chose to make excuses for them or overlook them. I didn't notice they were becoming more frequent and more hurtful. And when I did, I couldn't just flip a switch and stop loving him. Love, or whatever it was that I felt for him, is a strong emotion, and emotions don't take orders from your brain. Changing your emotions takes time. For me, it took months to get over Seth, even after I'd left.

When people ask me, "Why didn't you leave?" I want to tell them it wasn't that simple because leaving was hard, and I was in love. But I know they won't understand. They'll chalk it up to Stockholm syndrome, where a person falls in love with their captor or abuser. But that's not it. I was in love with Seth before any of the bad stuff. I didn't fall in love with him because of it. People who haven't been through a relationship like mine don't understand how difficult it is to make yourself stop loving a person, no matter how horrible the relationship becomes.

I've also heard comments like "That never happened to me because..." or "That *would* never happen to me because..." followed by an explanation of how they're too smart, too strong, or too savvy to fall for someone like Seth, much less stay with him. The truth is, that never happened to them because they were never targeted by a narcissist, or a sociopath, or anyone with a personality disorder. They never fell in love with a person who pretended to be normal and nice, then, over time, exposed another side of their personality, a side so unpredictable, so odd, so beyond what you expect from a normal human being that you don't know how to respond.

When people judge me, or when they judge anyone who's

been in an abusive relationship like mine, they are essentially revictimizing someone who's already been through enough trauma. I get it, though; people want to understand what happened to me, and they want to believe it could never happen to them. Because it's scary. But abuse can happen to anyone. I know that now, and I've forgiven myself for allowing Seth to put me through that hell.

Looking back, I don't know who I was back then. I don't recognize that woman. She is not the woman I am today.

* * *

One real mistake that I made, that caused me shame for a long time, was my first marriage. And my divorce. Jeff and I were so in love, and he wasn't a bad guy, and I wasn't a bad person either. We were too young to be married, too young to even know what we wanted in life. You can drive at sixteen or younger in most states, vote at eighteen, and buy alcohol and cigarettes at twenty-one. But moving in with someone at eighteen and committing to spending the rest of your life with that person at the tender age of twenty-two—with sixty or seventy years ahead of you—seems slightly crazy. Some people make it work, and kudos to them. I don't know how they do it. I'm no longer ashamed of that marriage or the divorce. I was a kid.

After Brent and I were married, he told me that his first wife had had an affair during his second deployment, and that's what caused their separation. He was still trying to make the marriage work that second time we met, when our relationship began. But after that night, he said, he knew it was over with her, and he called her to tell her so.

Marriage isn't easy, no matter how much you love a person. It takes more than a teenager's commitment. It takes work. I simply wasn't mature enough to be married, and neither was Jeff. So, I have no feelings of guilt at all about that time in my life. As for all the other mistakes, well, I'm still working on those. And I'm making progress.

* * *

I'm most proud of the mother I've become. Brent and I treat one another with love and respect. We put each other first. We want our children to see what a healthy relationship looks and feels like. We are their role models, and we want them to grow up and have healthy relationships too.

My children's experiences are completely different than what mine were at their ages. You might say they're the exact opposite. I grew up in fear, feeling unwanted and unloved. Now, in my home, Brent, Zechariah, Harper, Otto, and I tell each other "I love you" every single day. Not just once but all the time. My kids will often just run up to me and wrap their arms around my legs or put up their arms to be held and say, "I love you, Mommy!" Sometimes I tear up, hearing those words. I smother them in hugs and kisses, so grateful to have them in my life, and so grateful to have love to give them too. Grateful to be a person who gets more satisfaction from loving others than from anything else I can do.

There's no unpredictability. We have schedules because I want my kids to know what's coming instead of being afraid of what might happen. I talk to my kids a lot. We're big on communication. Talking to them goes a long way toward preventing the need to correct them after they mess up. They aren't perfect, and I don't expect them to be. Sure, we have punishments: timeouts, along with explanations for the punishment. And solutions, so they don't make the same mistakes again: "You're in timeout for five minutes because you called your sister a name. Next time she makes you angry, tell her what she did and how it made you feel. If you're too upset to discuss it, go to another room and settle down. Give yourself a timeout, then come back and talk about it."

Kids are smart. If you give them the tools to solve their own problems, they will use them. And they'll feel good about themselves instead of feeling shame.

Finally, I protect my children from people who can hurt them. Not just physically, but harm them with harsh words, shaming, and lies. Harm them with broken promises. Doing anything that fills them with feelings of confusion and distrust. I keep them away from Jennie. Even though she's their biological grandmother, they are better off without her in their lives.

I have more work to do on myself, but being a good mom is my proudest achievement. It really is the hardest job in the world, but it's the best job too. Moms who get it right put a lot of love into their children, and that love doesn't stop with them. It's passed on to their children's children, and their spouses, and everyone else they care about. That love goes out into the world, making it a better place for everyone. We put moms on a pedestal, but the truth is, the ones who get it right deserve to be there.

Conclusion

I'M NOT PERFECT. THERE ARE DAYS WHEN I STILL GET angry. Sometimes I just want to yell because that's what I was taught. Even though I know better, it's a day-to-day struggle, but it's one I'm winning. With the support of my friends and my family, I've become a woman who can give and receive love. I'm a mother, wife, sister, daughter, and now, a friend to other women who've experienced similar betrayal and suffering.

I needed help to get here. I had to put aside my fears, reach out to the right people, and be vulnerable. That was the most difficult part of all. But talking about my past, with my husband and in talk therapy with my doctor, was the bright light that cut through the darkness and led me to where I am today.

The more I talk about my past, the more women I meet who had similar experiences. Some of these women are friends I've known for years, who never felt safe confiding in anyone before. Just knowing that they're not the only one helped them open up.

I hope that if you're a girl living with an abusive mother, you find some hope in my story. It doesn't have to be this way.

There is a better life for you. For women who grew up with generational trauma, I hope you also find some hope here—hope that you can heal, and forgive, and have real, healthy relationships that look nothing like the ones you grew up with. These relationships may not exist in your household now, but they're out there. Look for them, reach out for them. Be open to them. You can create the healthy house, the warm, safe, comforting environment that you wish you had. The house you wanted to stay at every weekend growing up, like the one I found at my friend Sarah's, thanks to her mother, Jill.

If this book positively affects even one other woman, I will consider it a success. I want you to know that you're not the only one who had a bad mom. You're not the only one trying to break the cycle, to do better for yourself and your children.

But you can only become a good mom—and a good wife, friend, and human being—once you are good to yourself, once you see your value, your worth. When you feel better about yourself on the inside, you can be better for everyone around you.

Recognize that it's okay to let go of people who are not good for you. When I dropped the guilt of feeling like I needed to have a relationship with Jennie, it changed me as a person. That relationship brought me down, caused me anxiety, led to tears, anger, and even more guilt. I don't have to have that person in my life—and I don't have to be the person I was with her in my life.

Once I let go of that relationship, it freed up a lot of space emotionally. I could grow and breathe more freely. I had let go of a burden that never should have been placed on me.

It's not your responsibility to fix a problem you did not create. If somebody in your family abuses you, it's not on you to fix them. You are only responsible for yourself. Take pride in that; you have worth. You deserve to be happy and healthy. And you deserve to have a family you love, who loves you—whatever that family looks like.

A family doesn't have to mean a mom, daddy, and siblings. Happy families come in all shapes, sizes, and variations. Some people have stepchildren; I chose a parent who isn't my biological mom. You can find family anywhere. Friends, parents, the lady down the road who bakes you cookies every week—whoever you think fits best for you, who gives you what *you* need in your life.

If you're having trouble speaking with someone about your trauma, give them this book. Tell them, "This isn't my story, but it will help you understand me. Please read it, then let's talk."

And if you need more help, please check out the resources at the end of this book.

Talking about it is the first step, but opening the door to that conversation can be difficult. Use this book to open that door and start that conversation with your partner, your spouse, your best friend, or maybe your own children. Welcome them into your story and let them show you the compassion you deserve. Because I believe that you're a wonderful person, worthy of love.

That feeling and belief—knowing that you are worthy of love. Giving love and allowing yourself to *be* loved. It's the best feeling in the world, and every one of us deserves it. If I can get there, anyone can. Reach out. Open that door. The light and the love are on the other side, waiting for you. It's beautiful. And you deserve it.

Resources

IF YOU SEE YOURSELF IN MY STORY, IF YOU'RE DEALING with depression, abuse, or anything else like the things I talked about in this book, please know that you don't have to handle it alone. There are people out there who care about people like you—people like us. They want to help. Here are a few places to check out. You can contact them online, or call or text them.

National Domestic Abuse Hotline
1-800-799-SAFE (7233)
Text START to 88788
https://www.thehotline.org/

National Suicide Prevention Lifeline
1-800-273-8255
https://suicidepreventionlifeline.org/talk-to-someone-now/

Substance Abuse and Mental Health Services Administration (SAMHSA)
1-800-662-HELP (4357)
https://www.samhsa.gov/find-help/national-helpline

National Eating Disorders Association (NEDA)

Call: 1-800-931-2237

Text: 1-800-931-2237

https://www.nationaleatingdisorders.org/help-support/
contact-helpline

National Sexual Assault Hotline

Call: 1-800-656-4673

https://www.rainn.org/

Acknowledgments

MANY PEOPLE HAVE SUPPORTED ME IN THIS JOURNEY from the moment I decided to write this book until the last word was written. I want to thank those who have been there for me, not only during this time but also during the many years it took me to get to this place where I could finally put it all into words.

Thank you, first, to my husband, Brent, for all of your love and support in everything that I do and for helping me see there is a true, healthy love to be had.

Thank you to my children, Zechariah, Harper, and Otto, for pushing me to be the best person and mother I can possibly be. Having all of you in my life encouraged me to break the cycle.

Thank you, Daddy, for being there for me always. You have been and continue to be that solid rock who would never, ever leave my side.

Thank you to my brothers, Andrew and Philip, for riding this rollercoaster life alongside me. I always knew I could count on you for anything.

Thank you to Jill for all of the unconditional, patient,

never-ending, motherly love and for teaching me that there are healthy ways to be a mom and a grandma.

Finally, thank you, Kimberly, for ultimately saving me when I thought I had nothing to live for. You will forever be my special someone.

About the Author

EMILY LEWIS BOWERS was born in a small town in Florida. Raised by a mother who abused and then abandoned her, Emily recognized as an adult that she was caught up in a cycle of generational trauma. She set out to break that cycle and become a different mom than the one she had, and that her own mother had. Through the support of her family, her friends, her therapist, and a woman she unofficially adopted as her new mom, Emily learned to love herself and become the mother she deserved but never had as a child.

After several years of moving around the country with her now ex-military husband, Brent, Emily settled in Vero Beach, Florida. The couple currently resides there with their three young children and Great Pyrenees, Josie.

Made in the USA
Middletown, DE
11 August 2022

71164636R00097